Color By Number Coloring Book For Girls

This Color By Number For Girls belongs to:

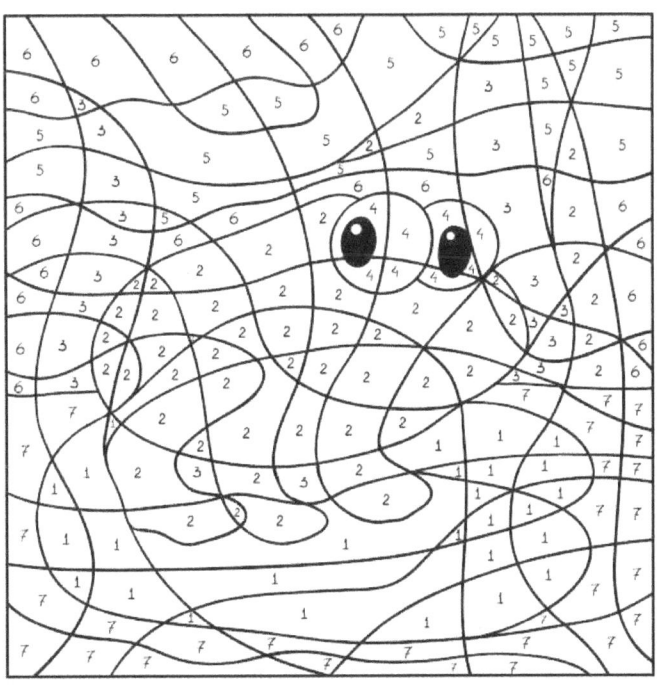

1 - light green 2 - green 3 - dark green 4 - white
5 - light blue 6 - blue 7 - dark blue

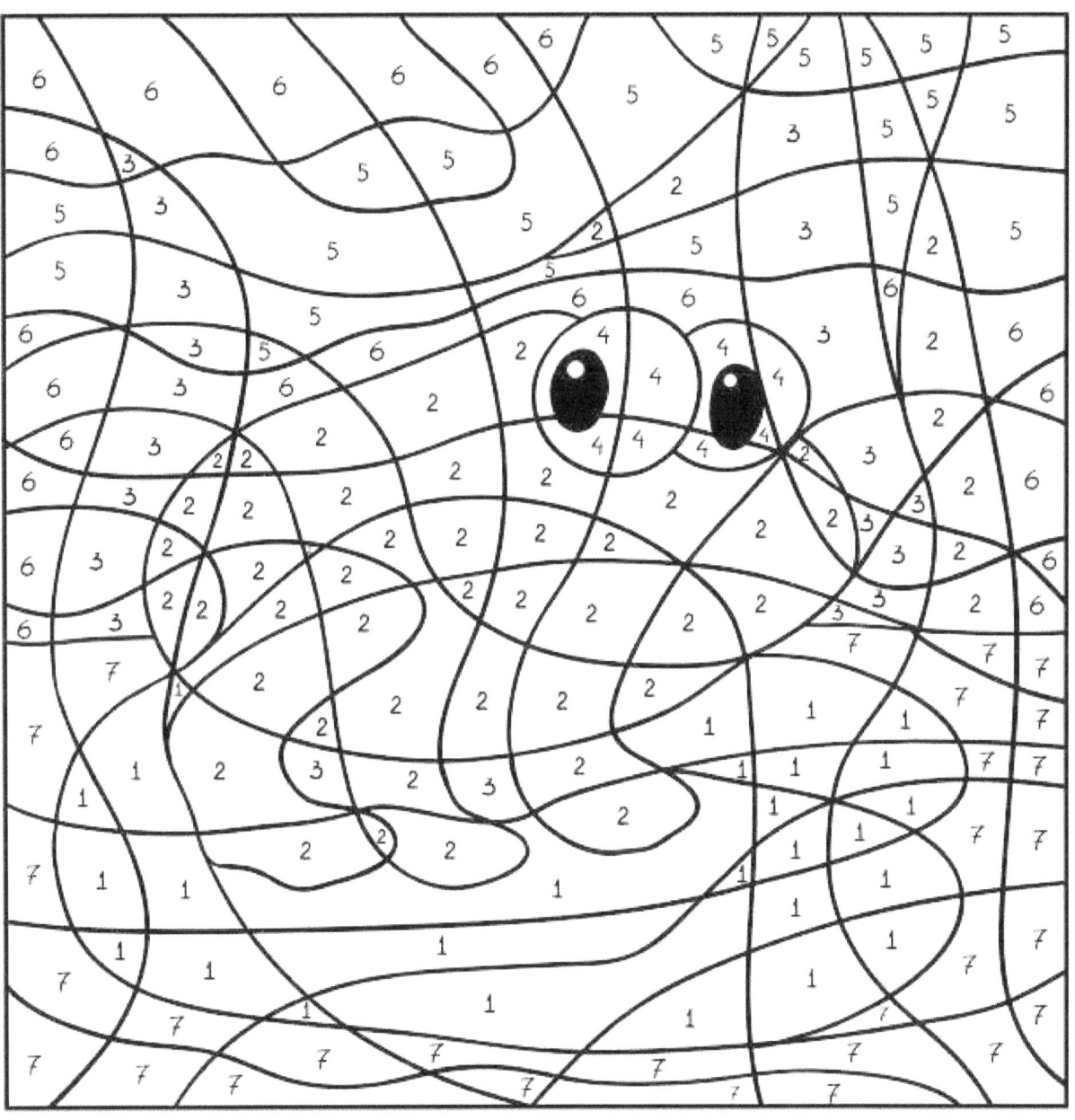

1 - light green   2 - green   3 - dark green   4 - white
5 - light blue   6 - blue   7 - dark blue

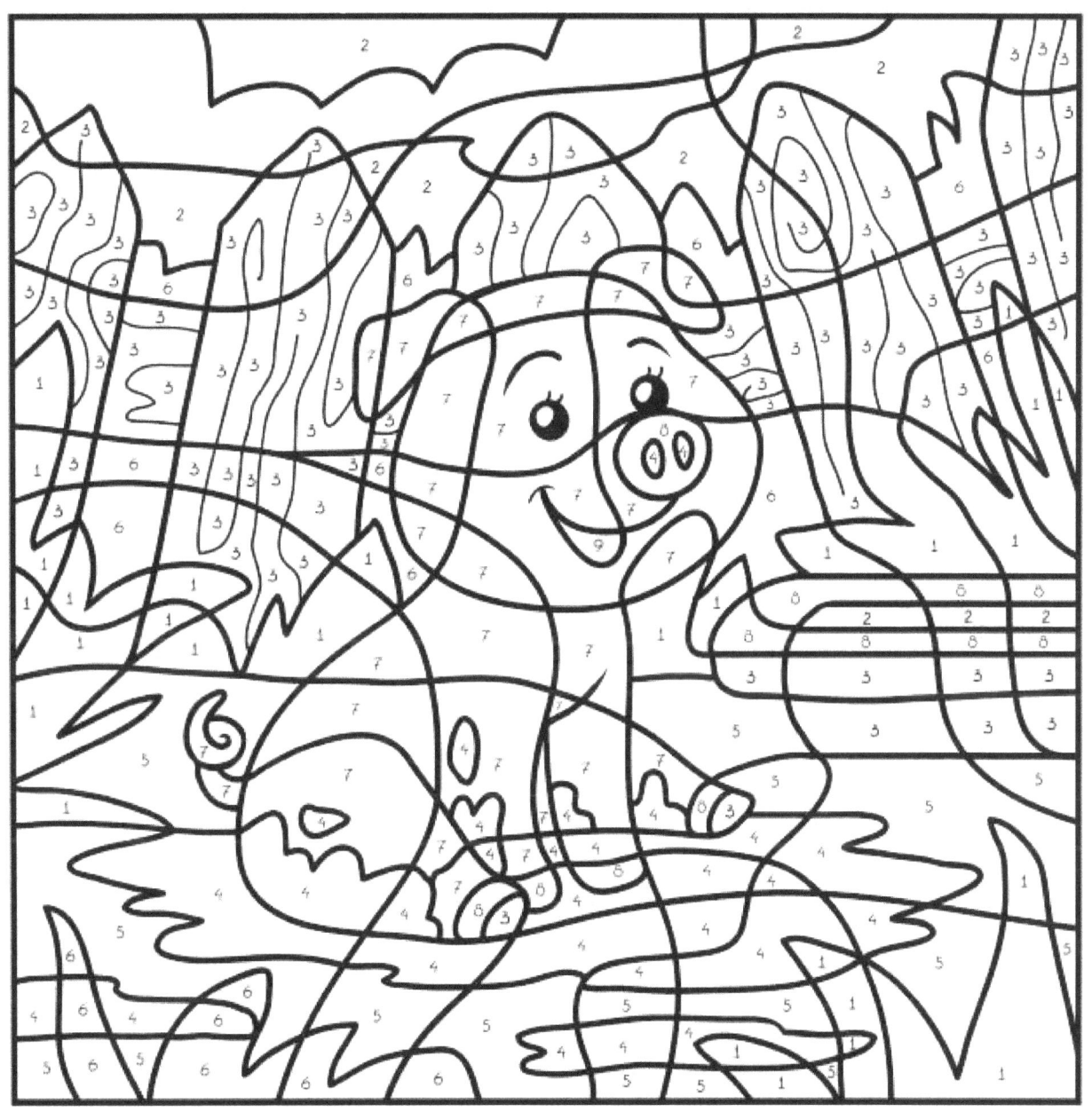

1 - green   2 - light blue   3 - brown   4 - gray   5 - yellow
6 - dark green   7 - pink   8 - orange   9 - red

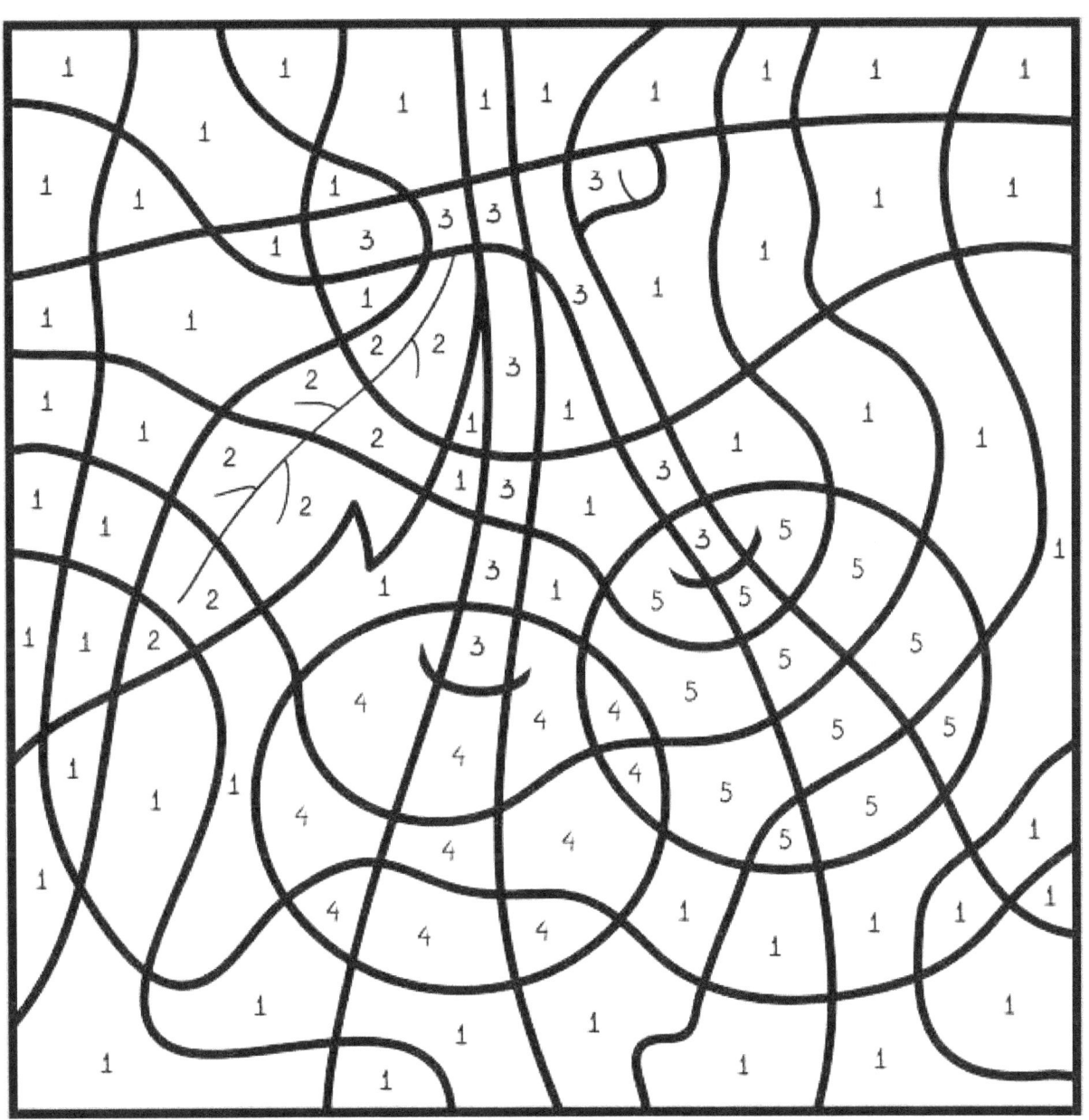

1 - light blue   2 - green   3 - orange   4 - red   5 - dark red

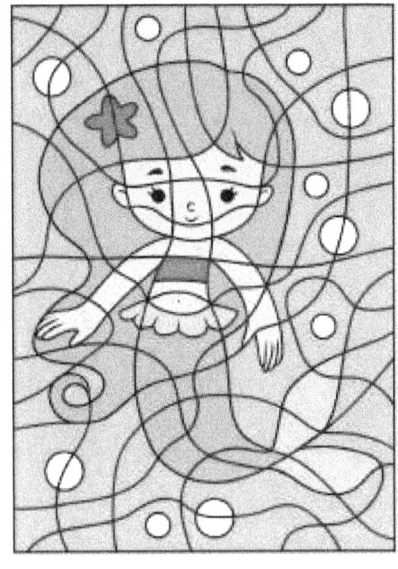

COLOR BY NUMBERS

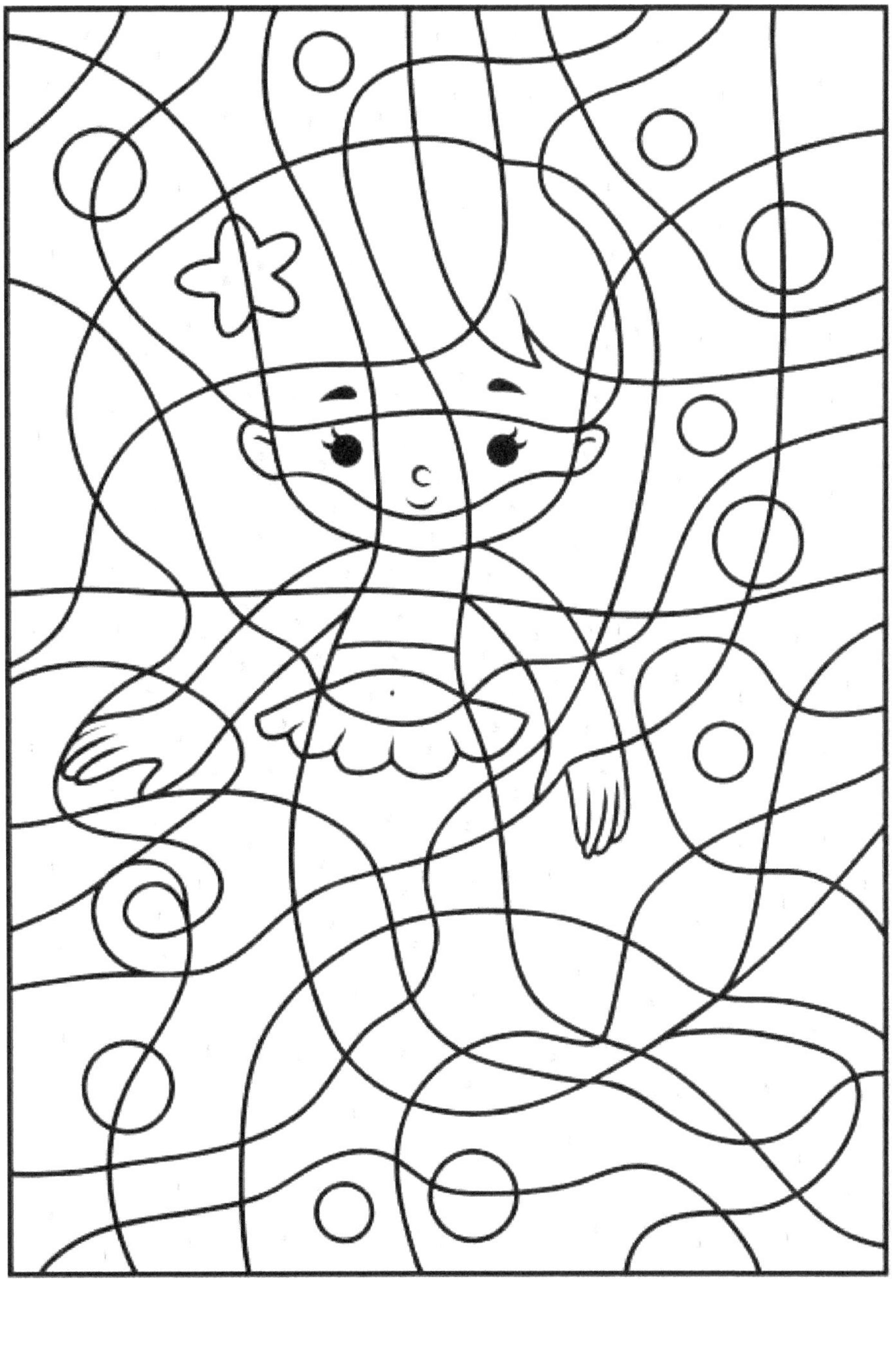

1 = BLUE

2 = GREEN

3 = YELLOW

4 = ORANGE

5 = PINK

6 = RED

Color by number

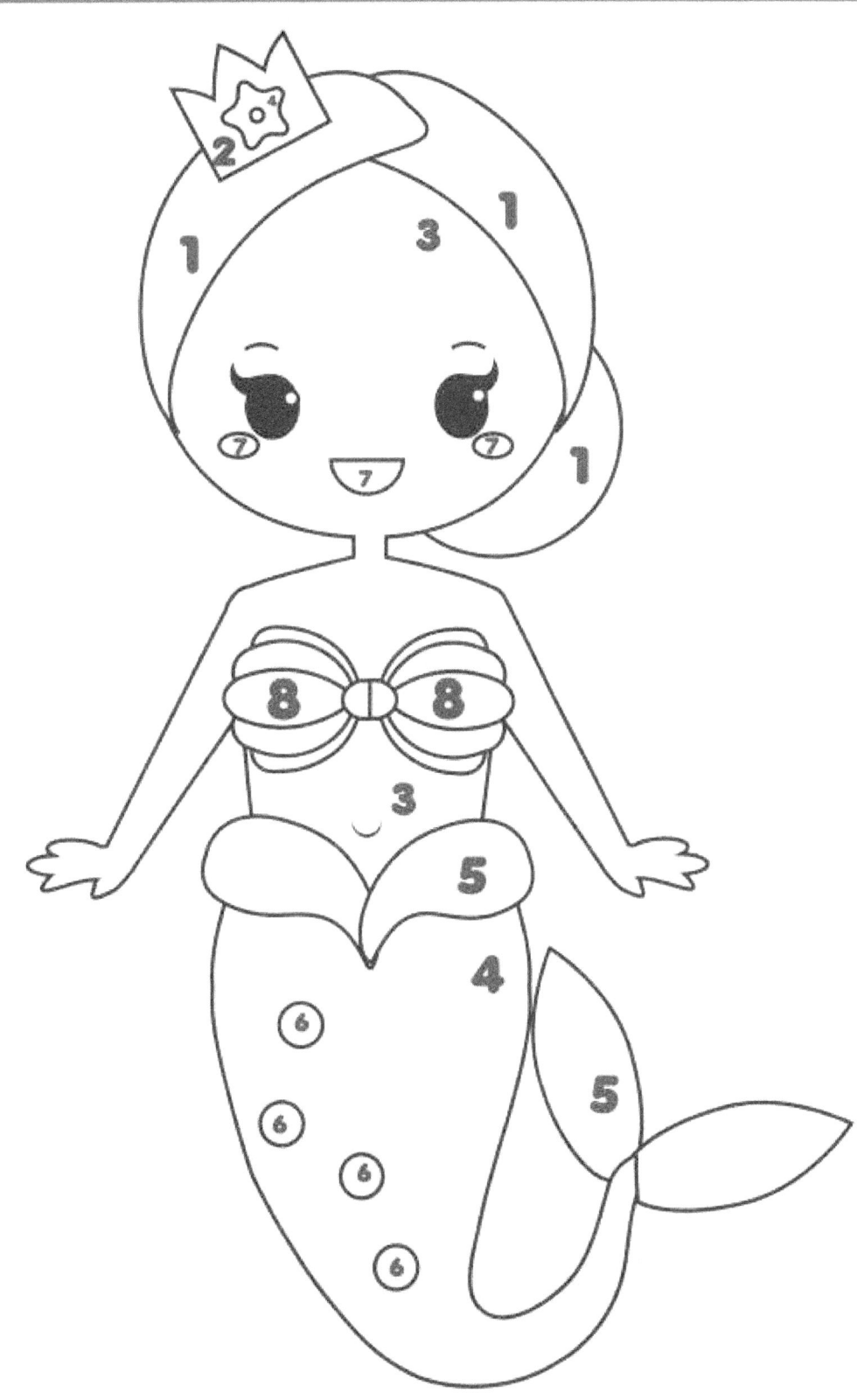

1 = ORANGE

2 = YELLOW

3 = BROWN

4 = LIGHT GREEN

5 = DARK GREEN

6 = BLUE

7 = PINL

8 = PURPLE

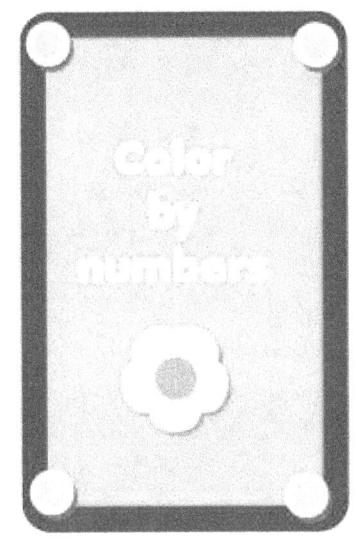

1 = BLUE

2 = LIGHT GREEN

3 = DARK GREEN

4 = ORANGE

5 = PINK

6 = YELLOW

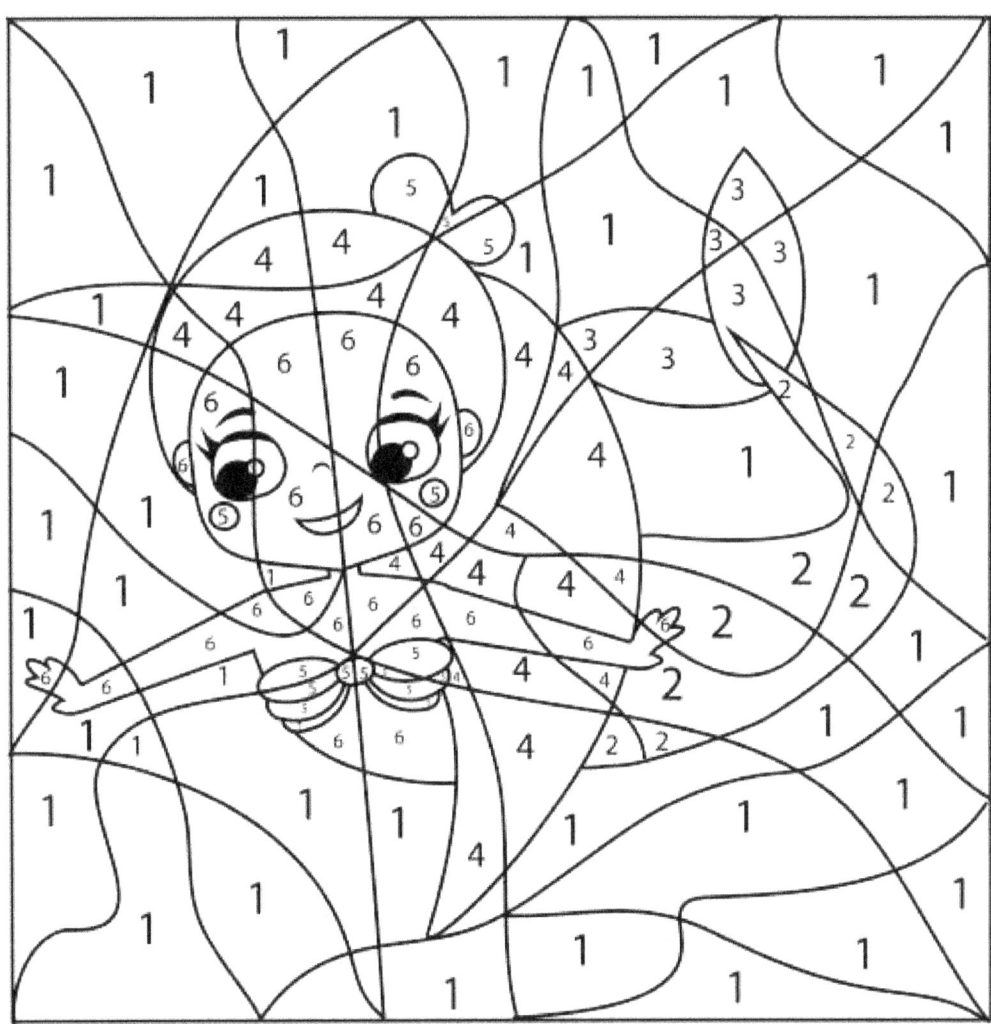

Color by numbers

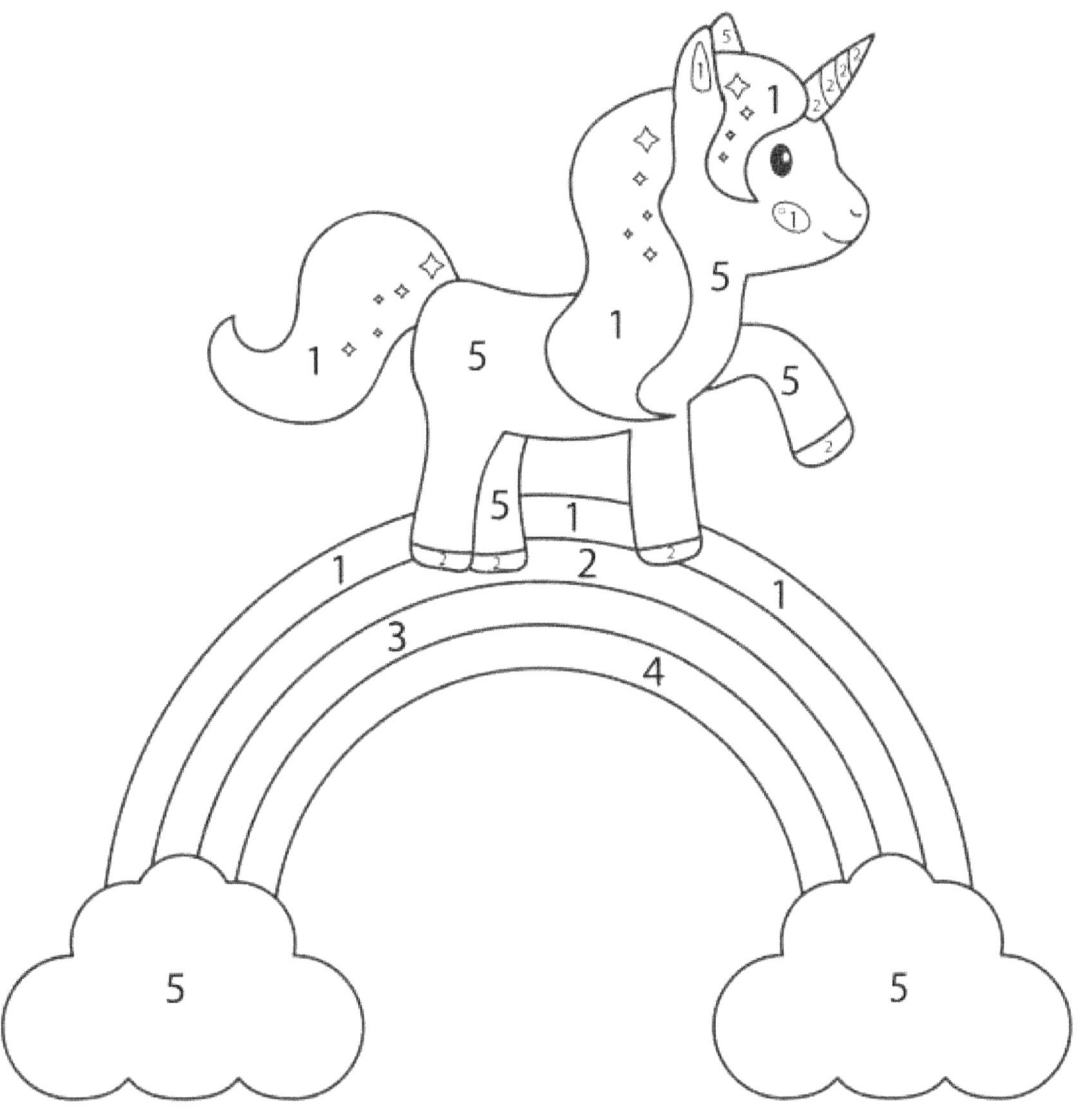

1 = PINK 2 = YELLOW 3 = GREEN 4 = BLUE 5 = WHITE

Color by numbers

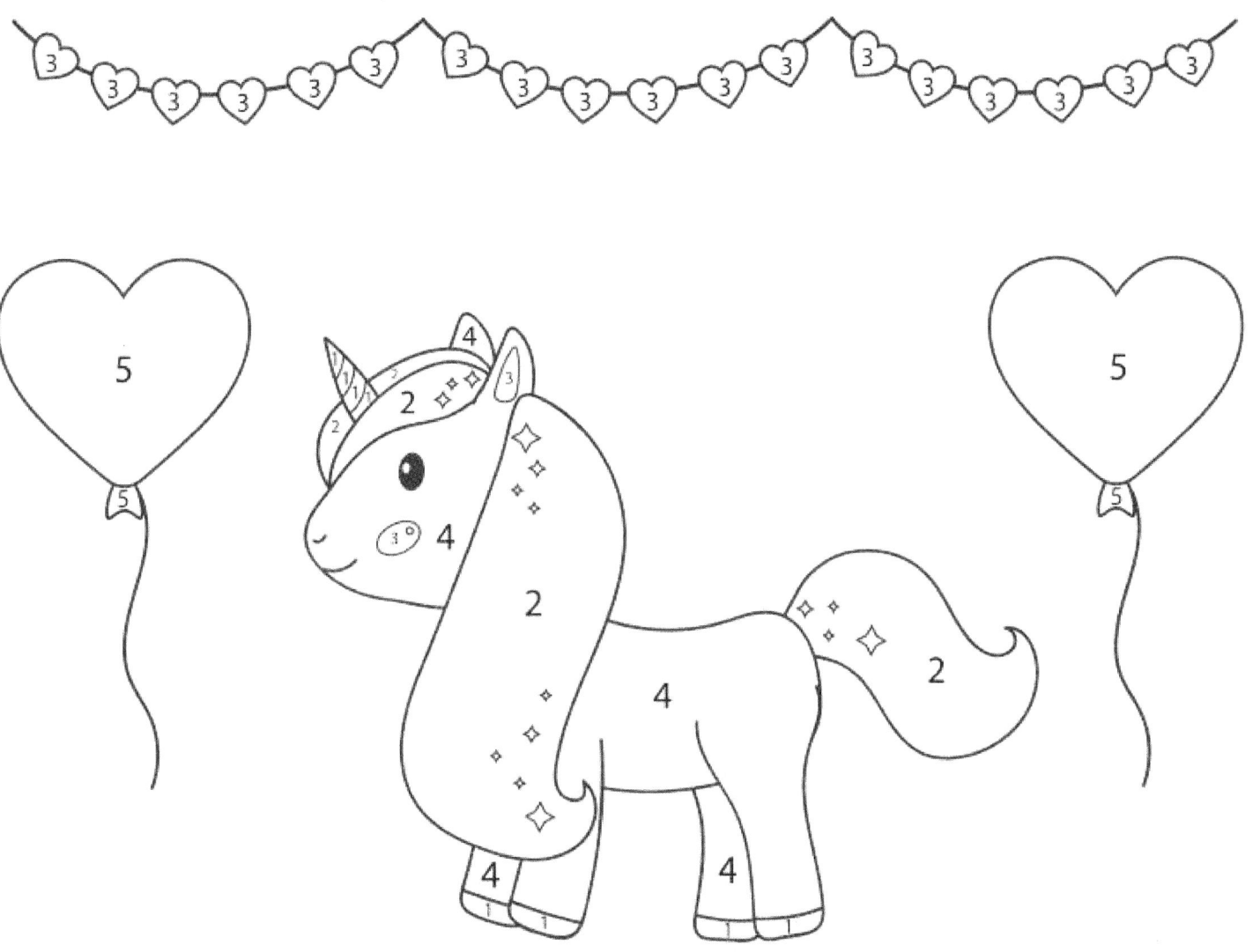

1 = YELLOW 2 = PURPLE 3 = PINK 4 = WHITE 5 = GREEN

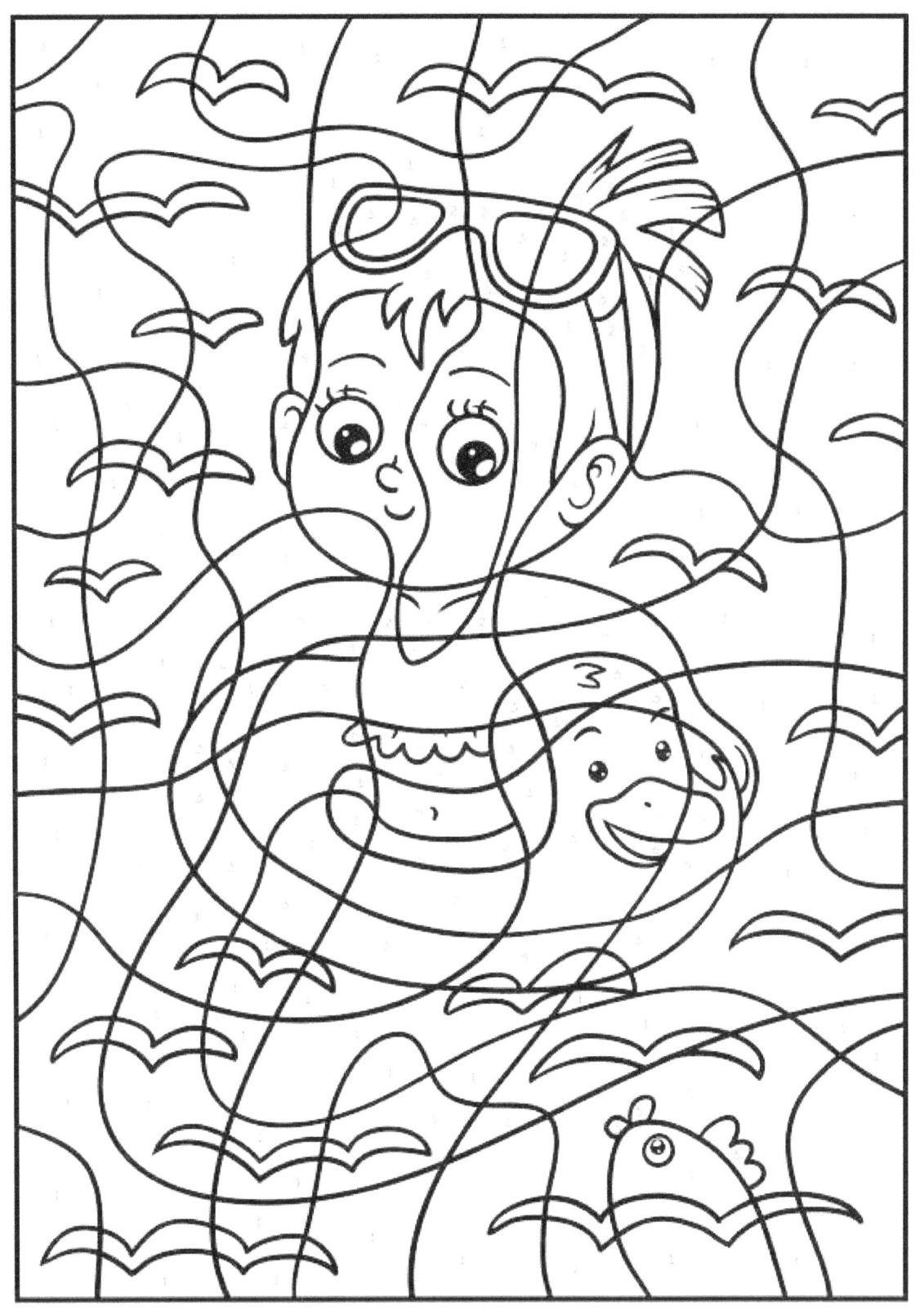

1 - light blue   2 - green   3 - yellow
4 - beige   5 - orange   6 - red

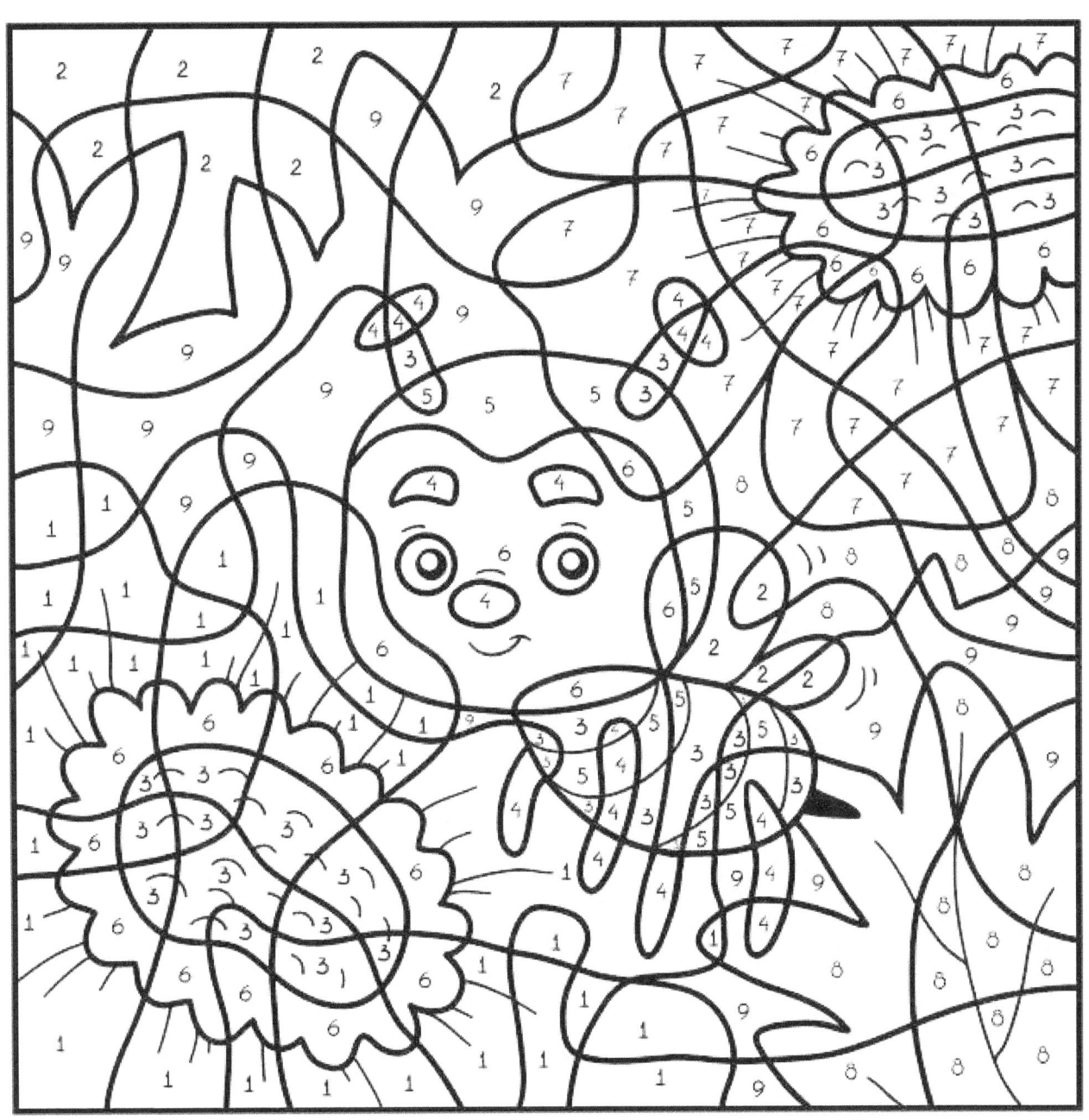

1 - red 2 - light blue 3 - yellow 4 - gray 5 - black
6 - beige 7 - pink 8 - green 9 - dark green

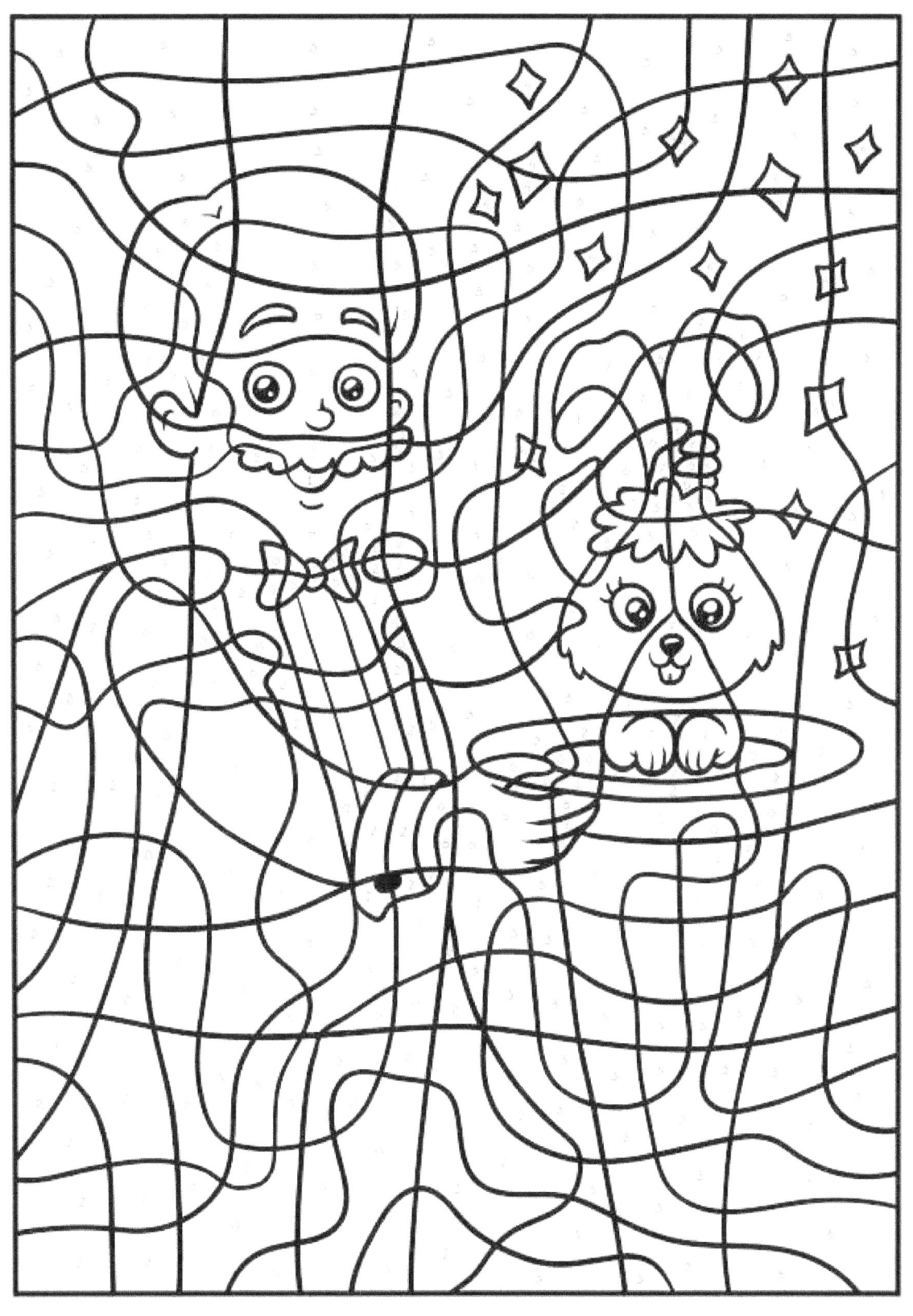

1 - pink 2 - purple 3 - blue 4 - yellow
5 - orange 6 - beige 7 - gray 8 - black

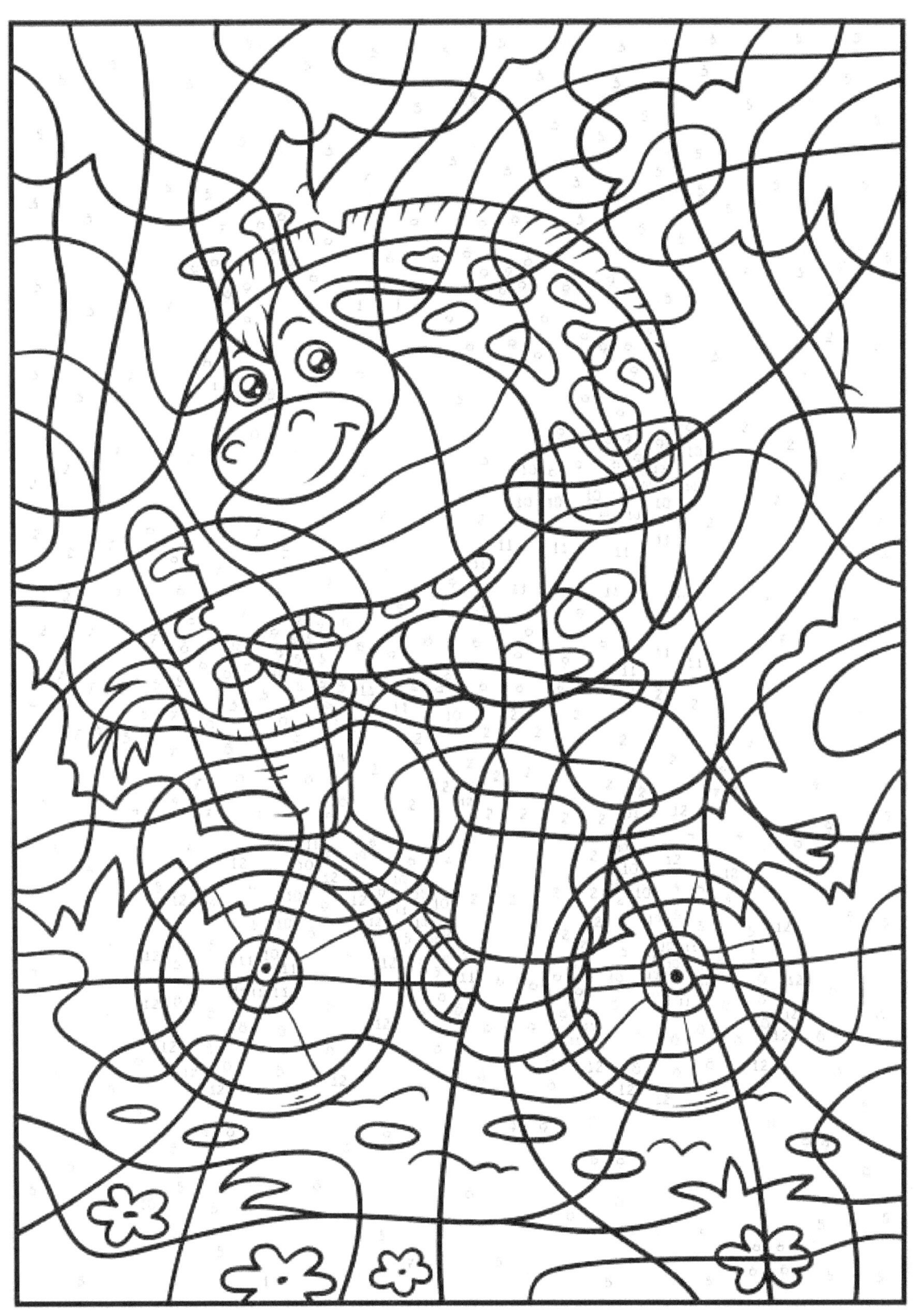

1 - pink   2 - blue   3 - light blue   4 - dark green   5 - green   6 - yellow
7 - orange   8 - beige   9 - brown   10 - red   11 - dark red   12 - black

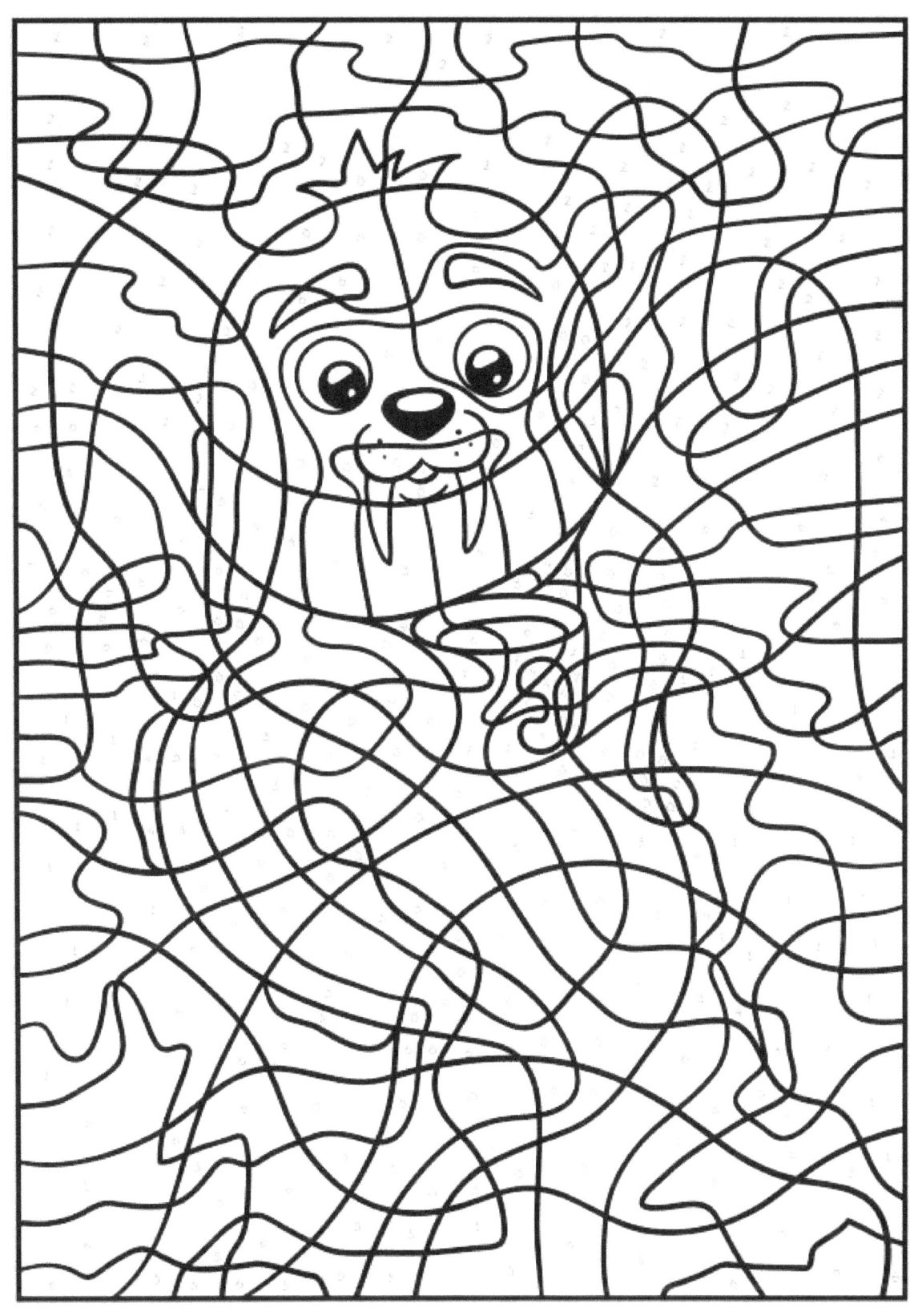

1 - blue   2 - light blue   3 - green   4 - yellow
5 - orange   6 - brown   7 - red   8 - gray

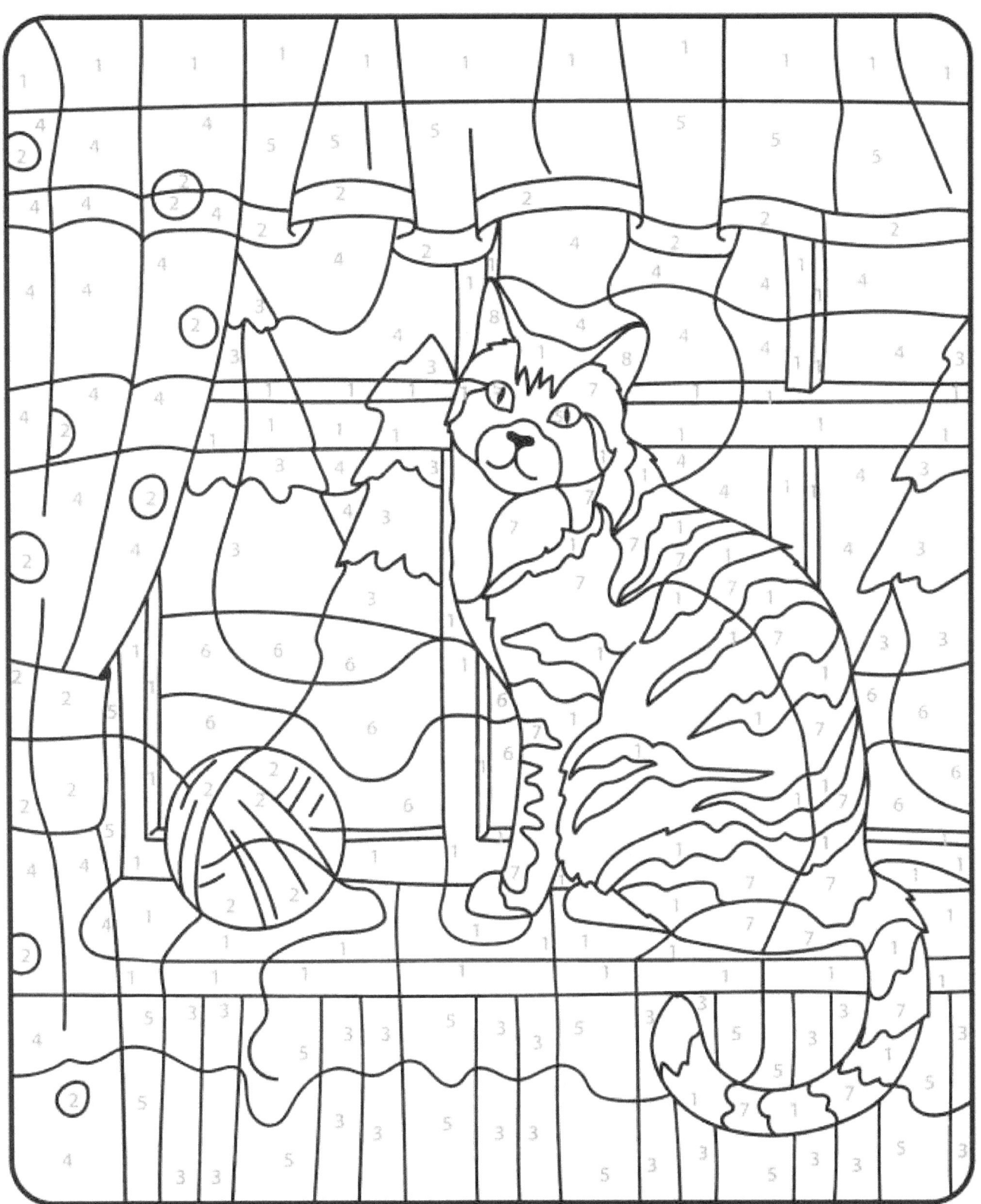

1. Beige   2. Red   3. Dark Green   4. Light Blue   5. Light Green   6. Light Brown
7. Dark Brown   8. Black

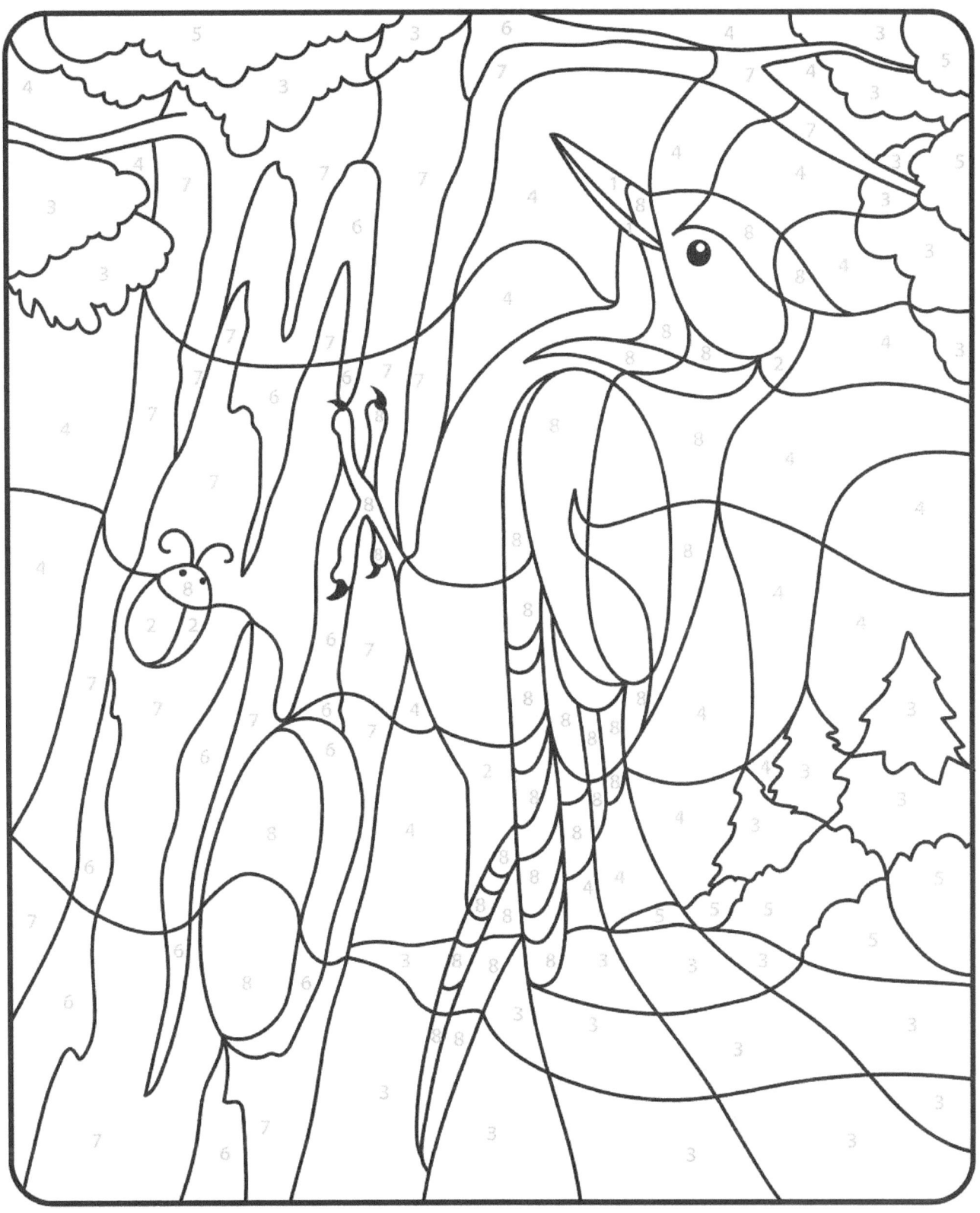

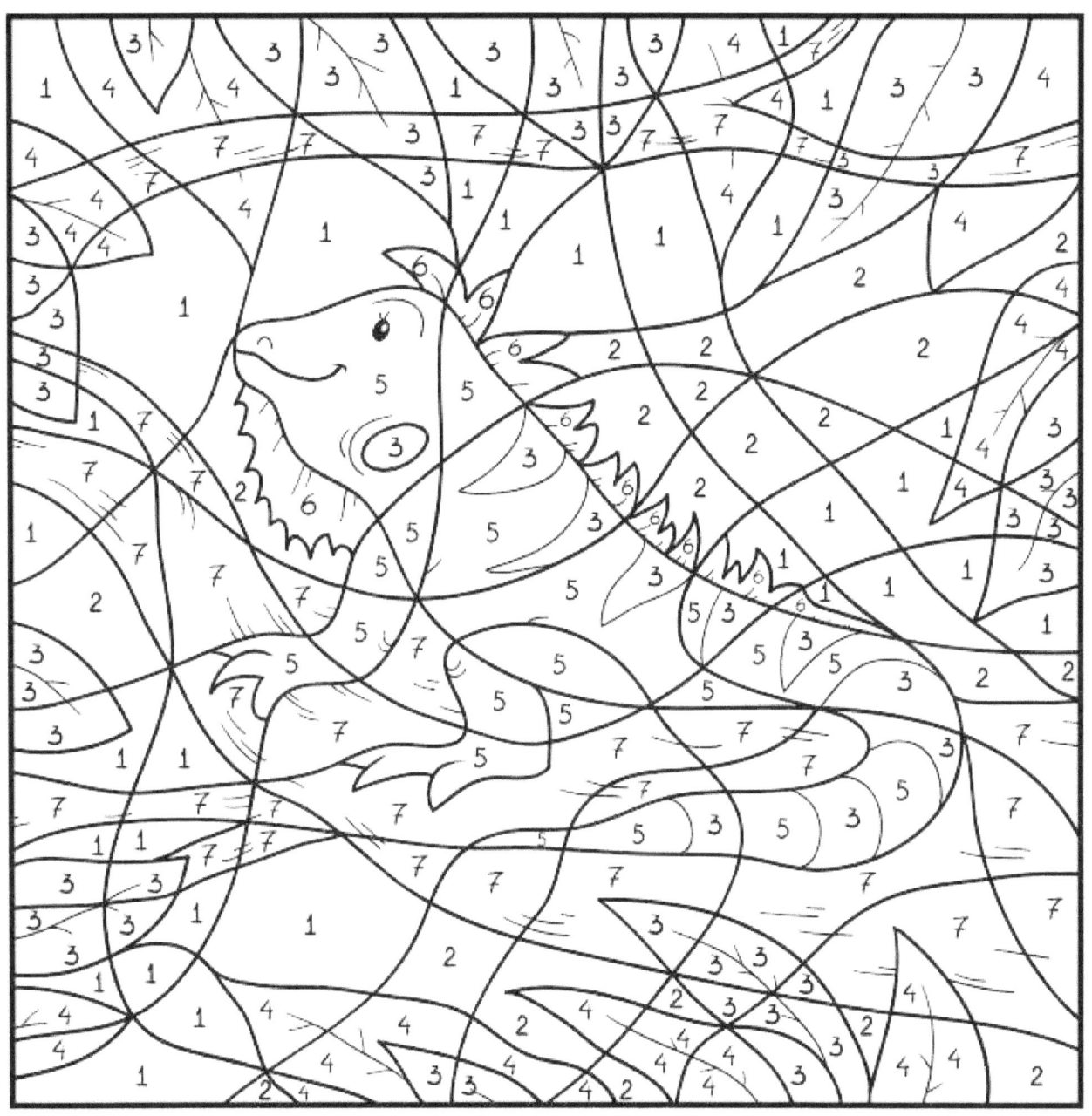

1 - light blue   2 - blue   3 - green   4 - dark green
5 - yellow   6 - orange   7 - brown

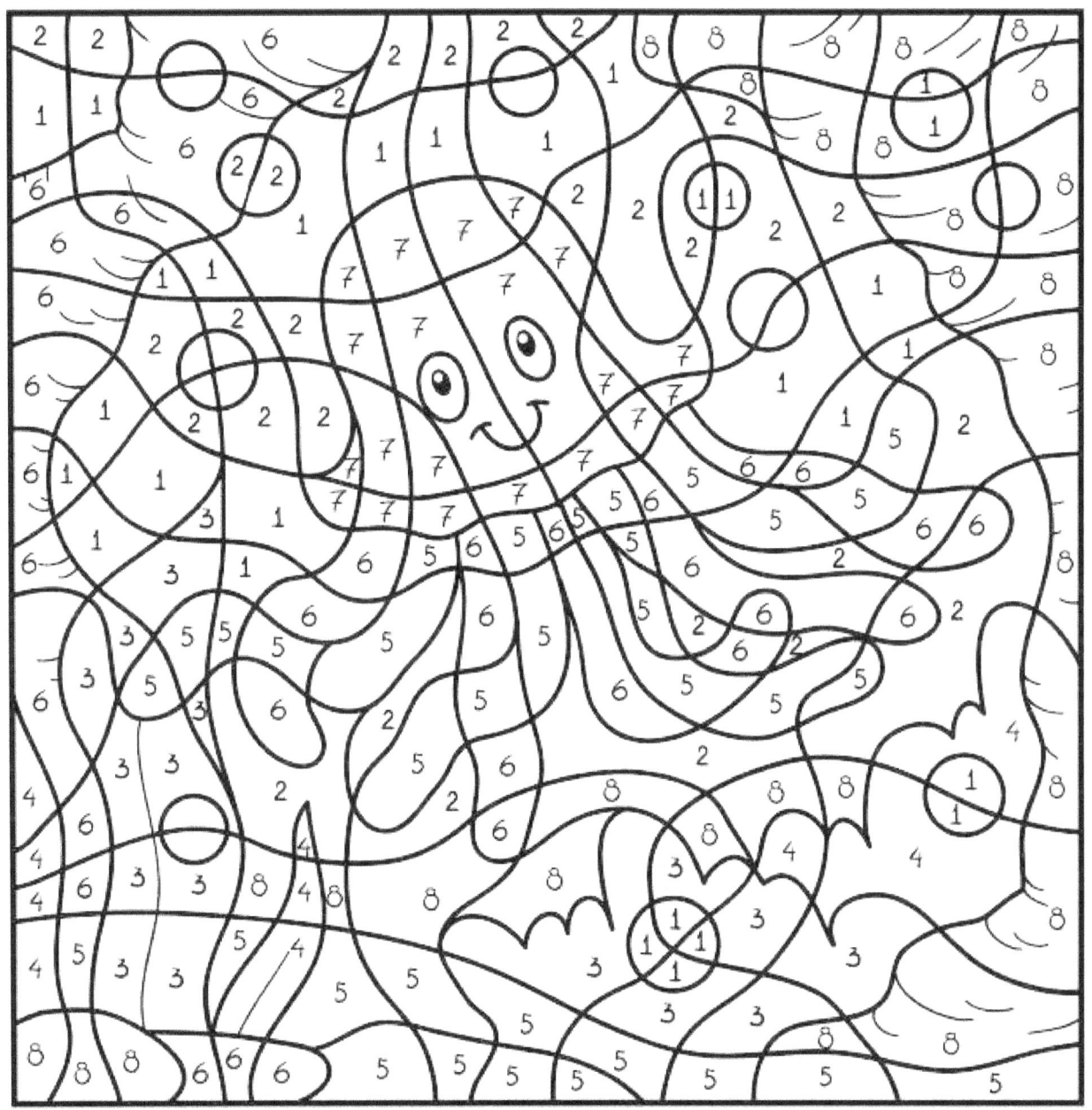

1 - light blue   2 - blue   3 - green   4 - dark green
5 - yellow   6 - orange   7 - pink   8 - brown

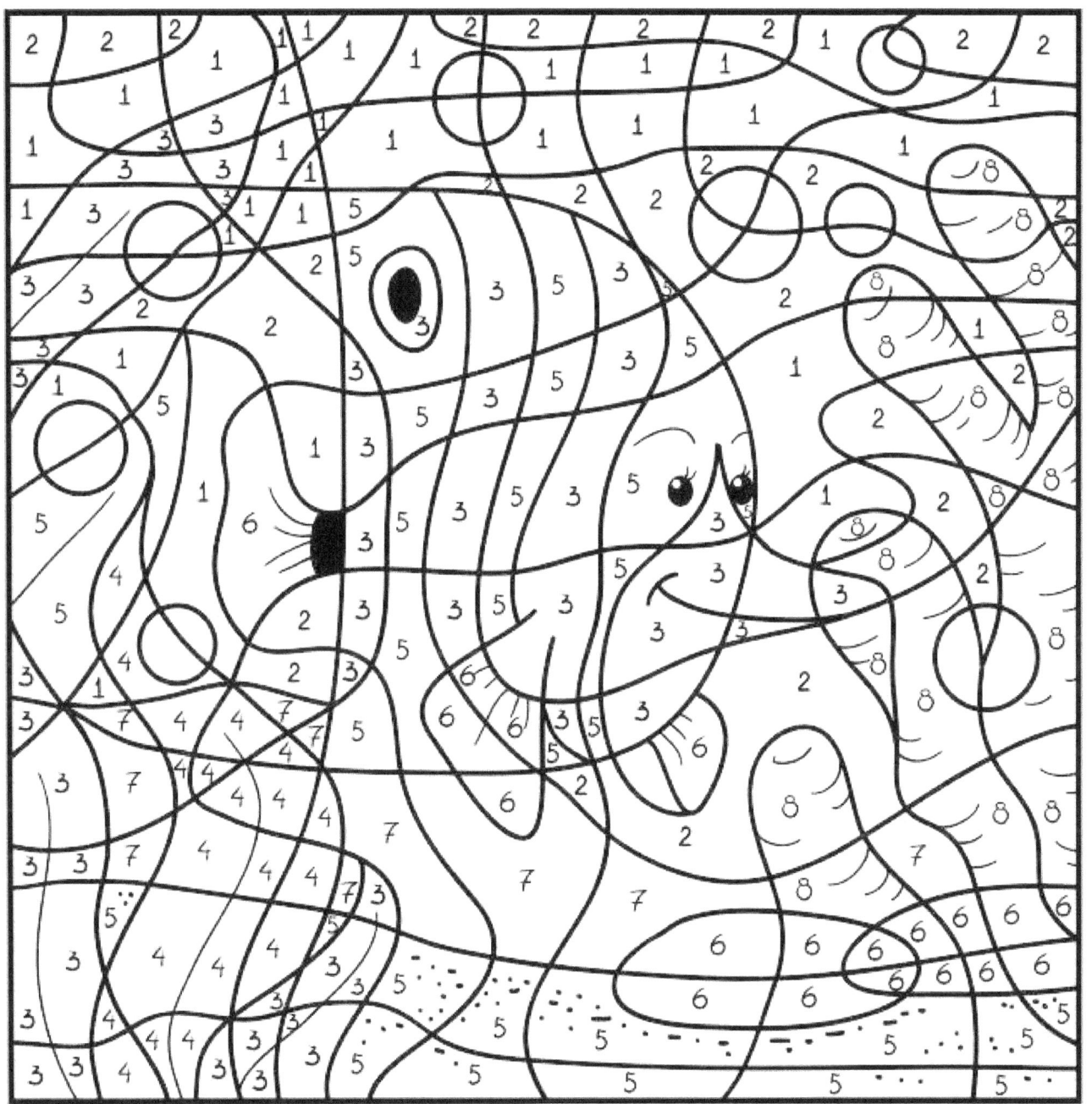

1 - light blue   2 - blue   3 - green   4 - dark green
5 - yellow   6 - orange   7 - brown   8 - pink

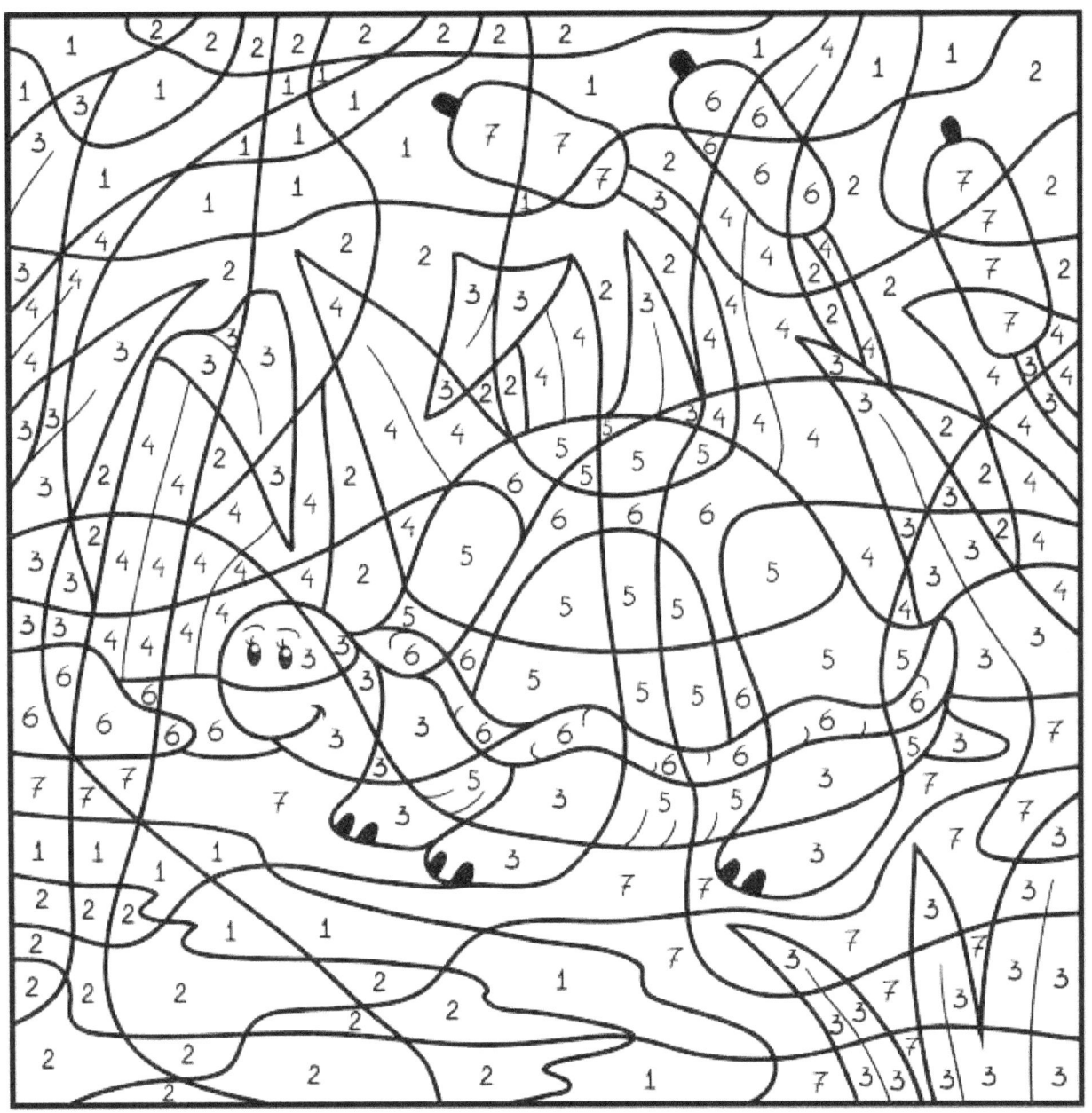

1 - light blue   2 - blue   3 - green   4 - dark green
5 - yellow   6 - orange   7 - brown

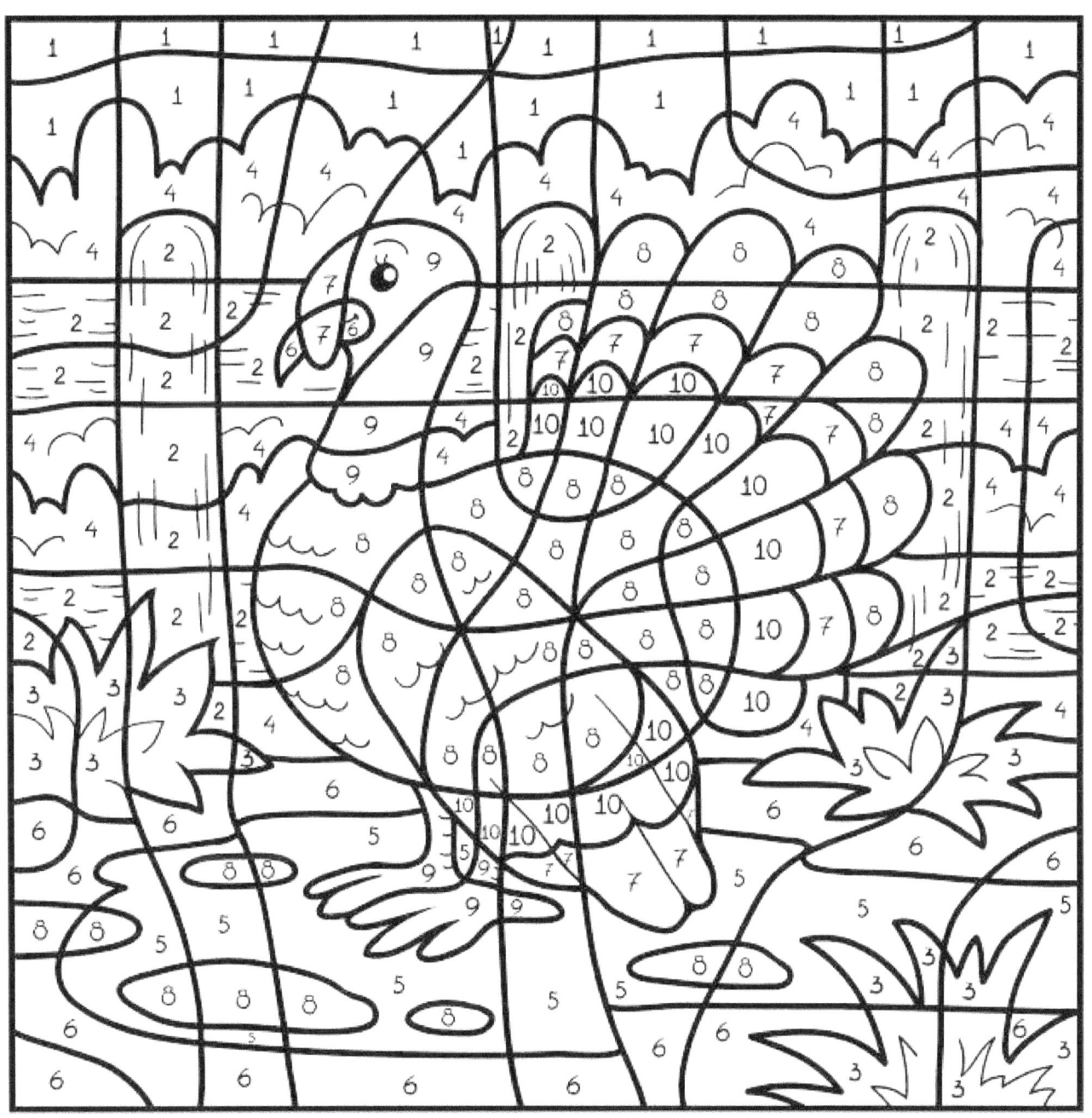

1 - light blue   2 - gray   3 - green   4 - dark green   5 - yellow
6 - orange   7 - red   8 - brown   9 - pink 10 - black

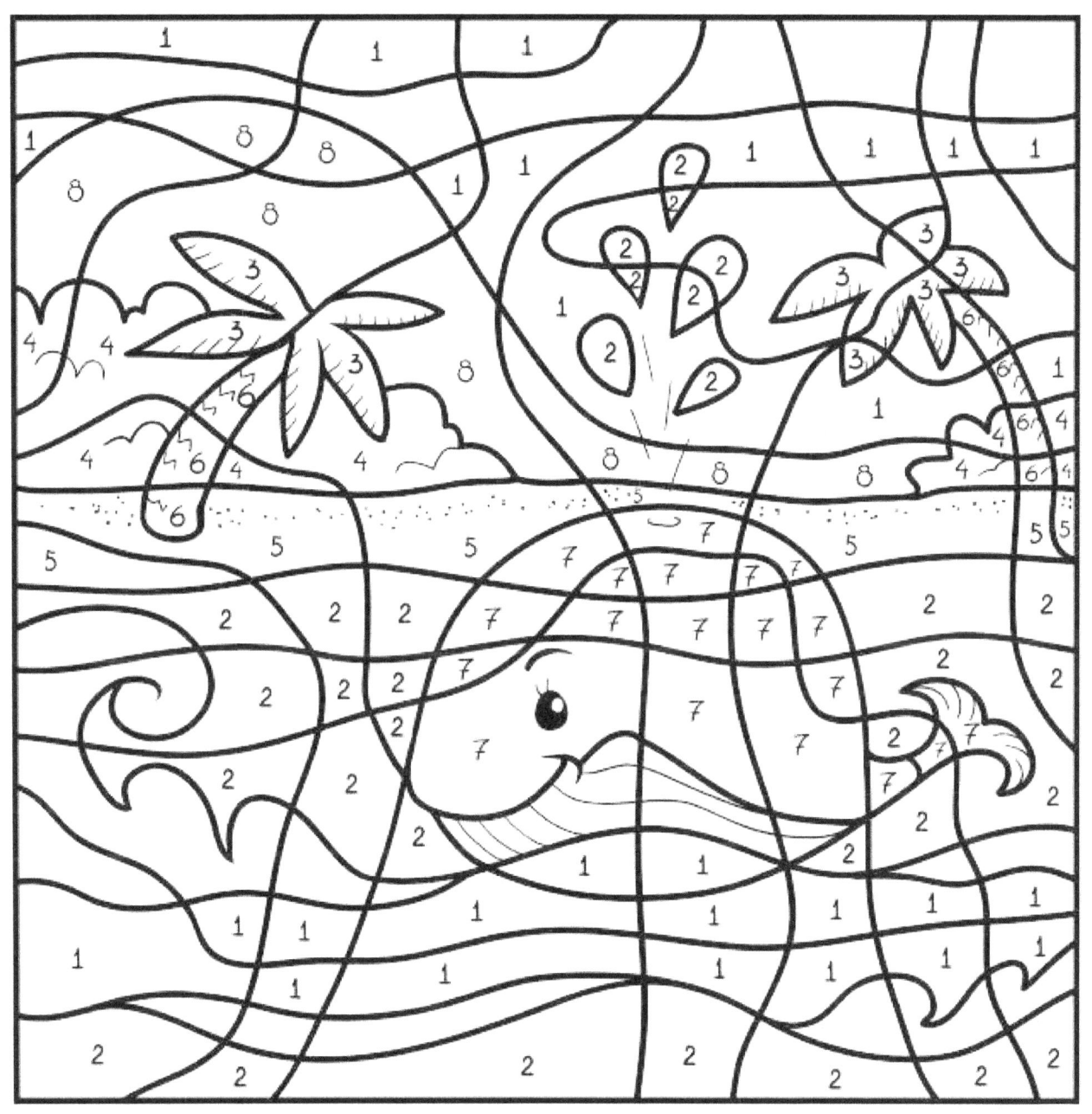

1 - light blue   2 - blue   3 - green   4 - dark green
5 - yellow   6 - orange   7 - gray   8 - brown

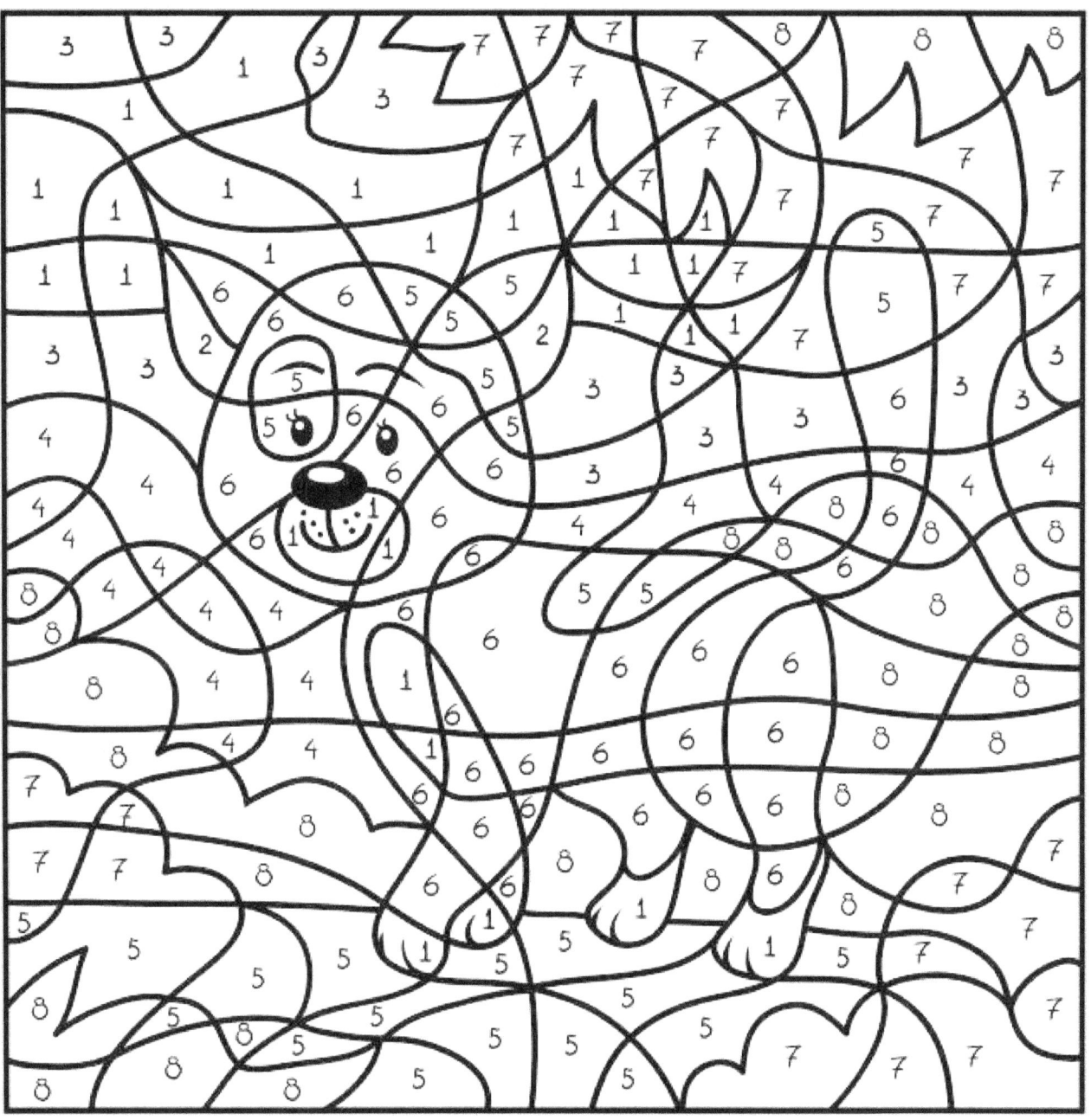

1 - white   2 - pink   3 - light blue   4 - blue
5 - yellow   6 - orange   7 - green   8 - dark green

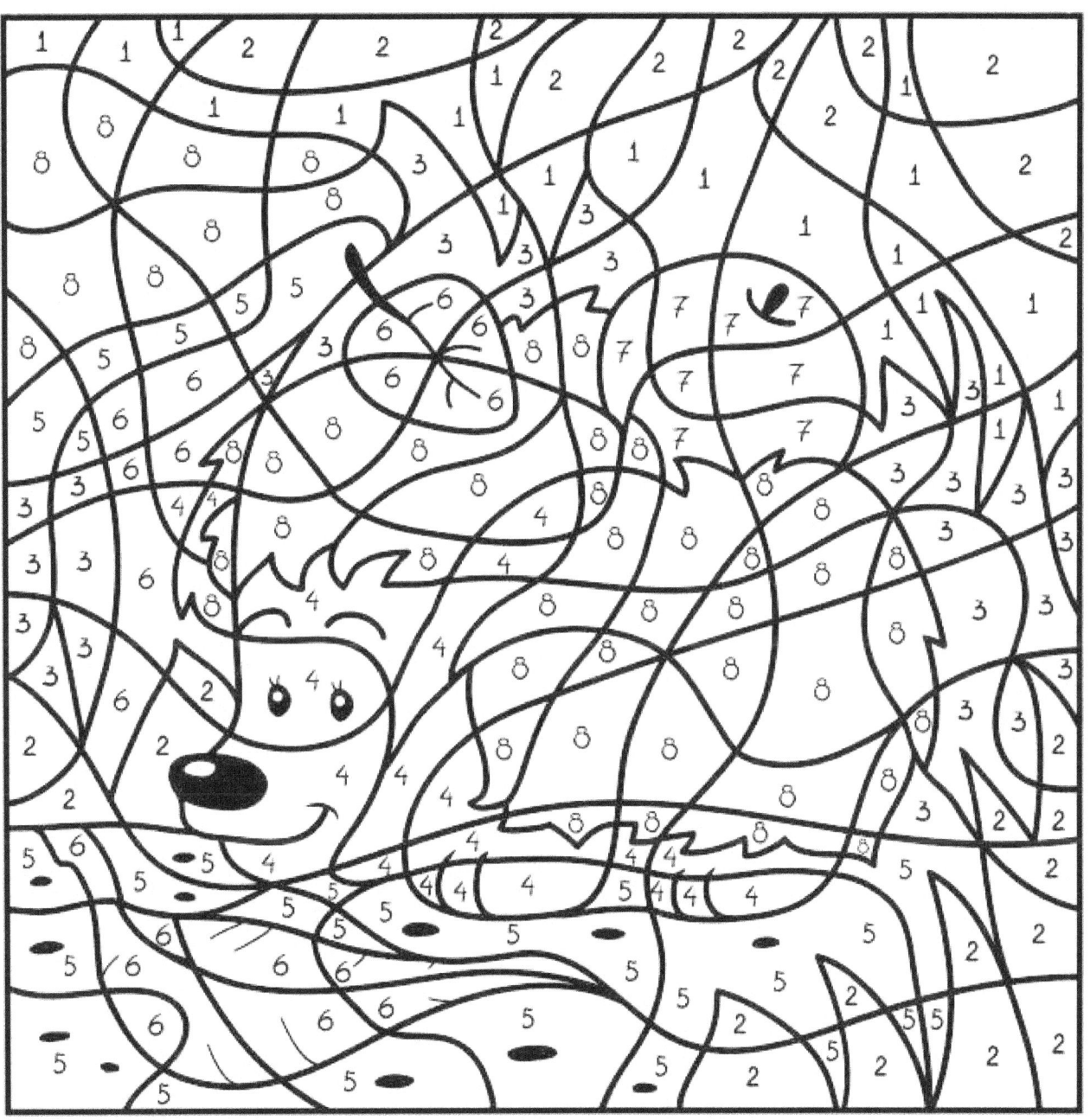

1 - light blue   2 - green   3 - dark green   4 - gray
5 - beige   6 - orange   7 - red   8 - brown

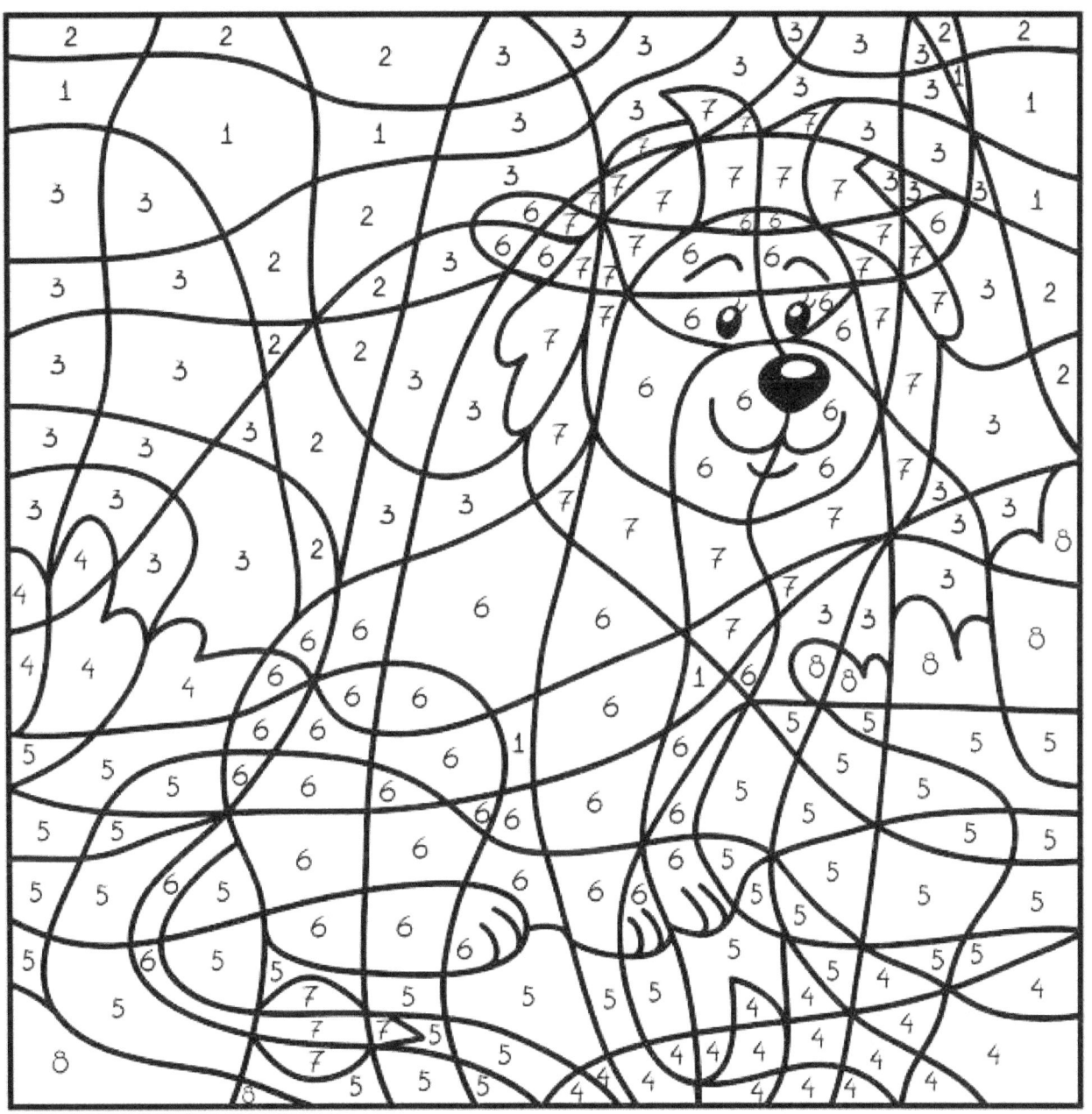

1 - white   2 - light blue   3 - gray   4 - green
5 - yellow   6 - orange   7 - brown   8 - dark green

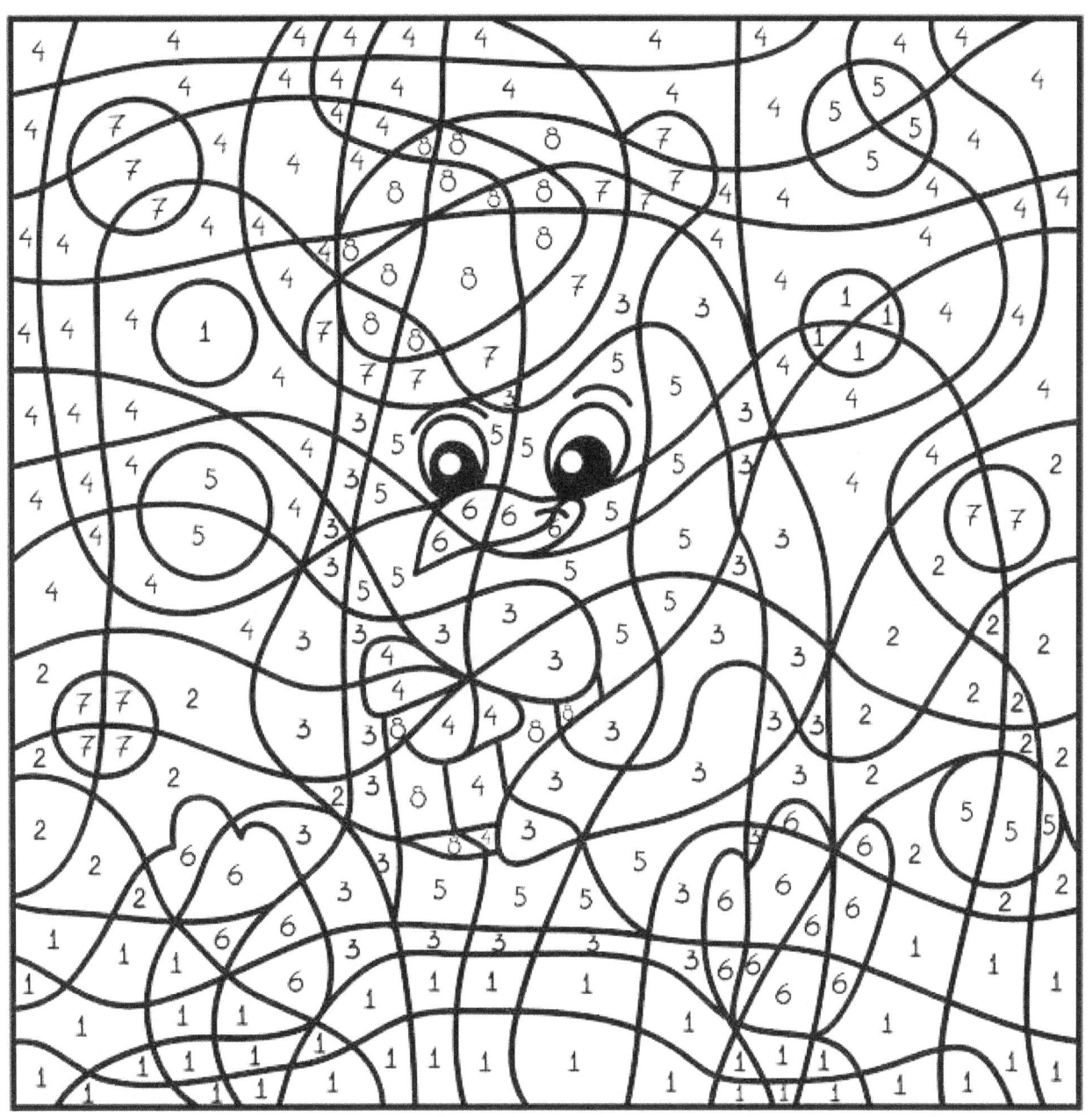

1 - light blue   2 - blue   3 - black   4 - dark blue
5 - yellow   6 - orange   7 - pink   8 - red

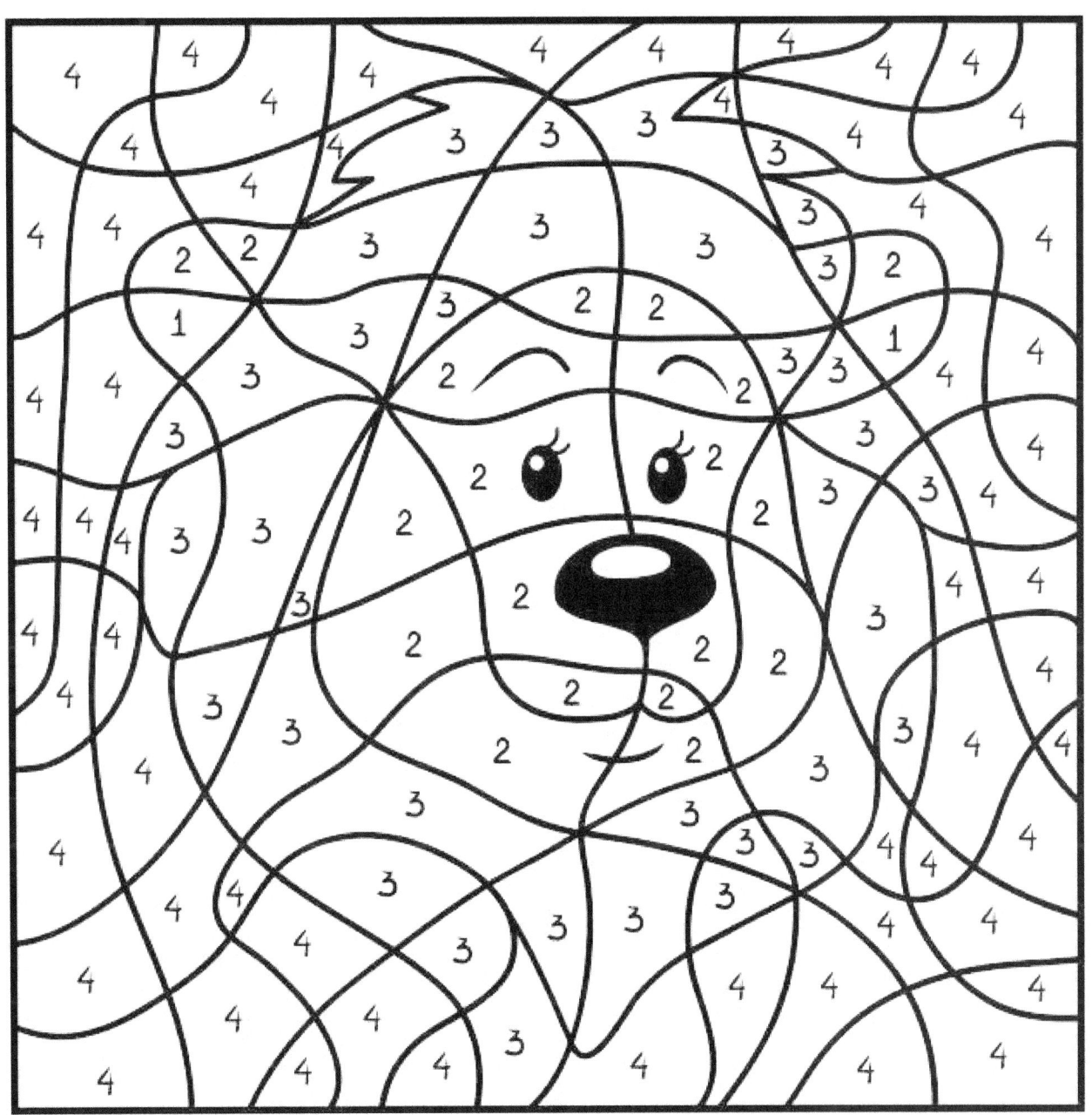

1 - pink   2 - yellow   3 - brown   4 - green

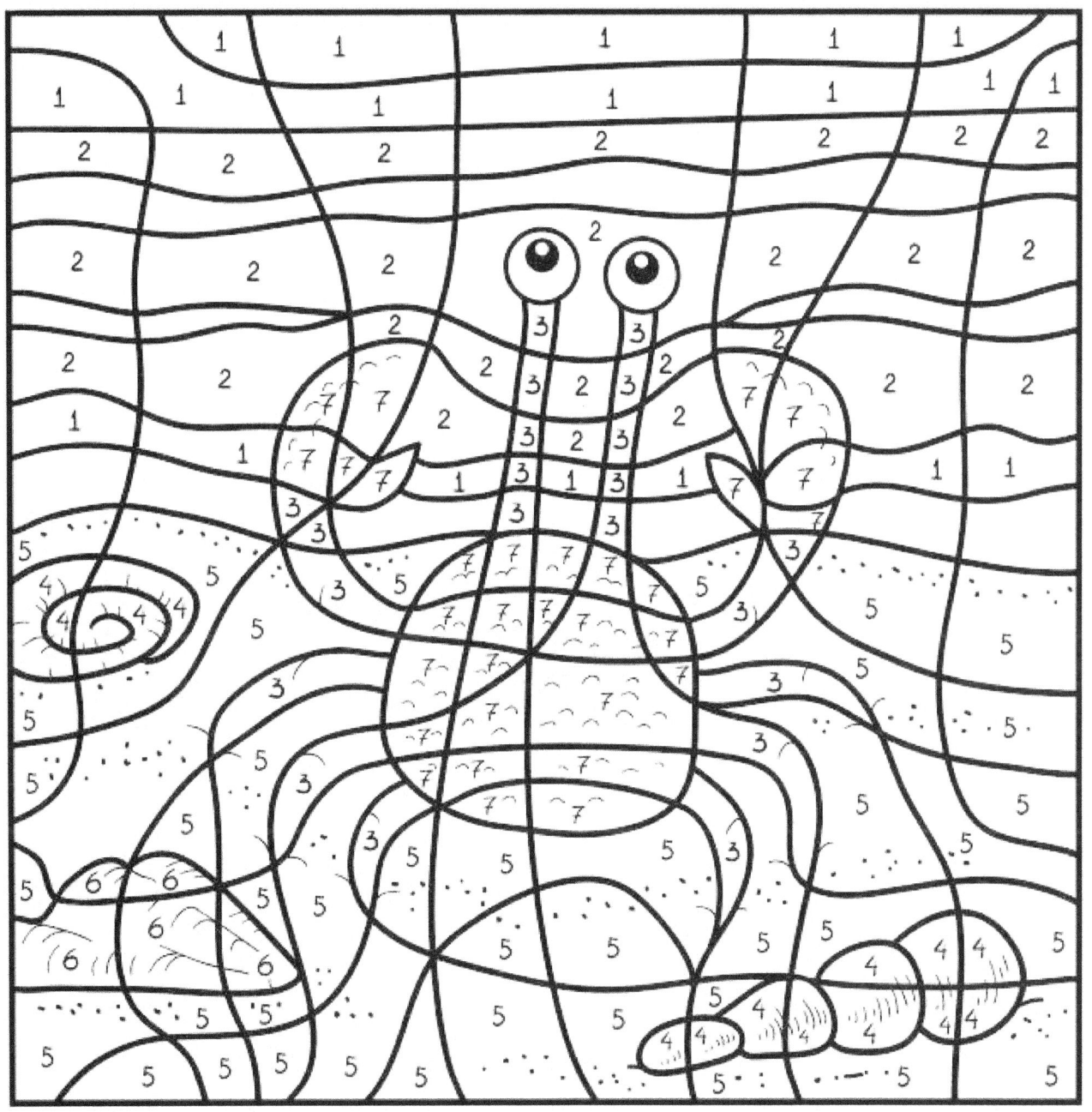

1 - light blue 2 - blue 3 - brown 4 - pink
5 - yellow 6 - orange 7 - red

1. Yellow   2. Red   3. Olive Green   4. Light Green   5. Dark Green   6. Pale Blue   7. Pink   8. Blue

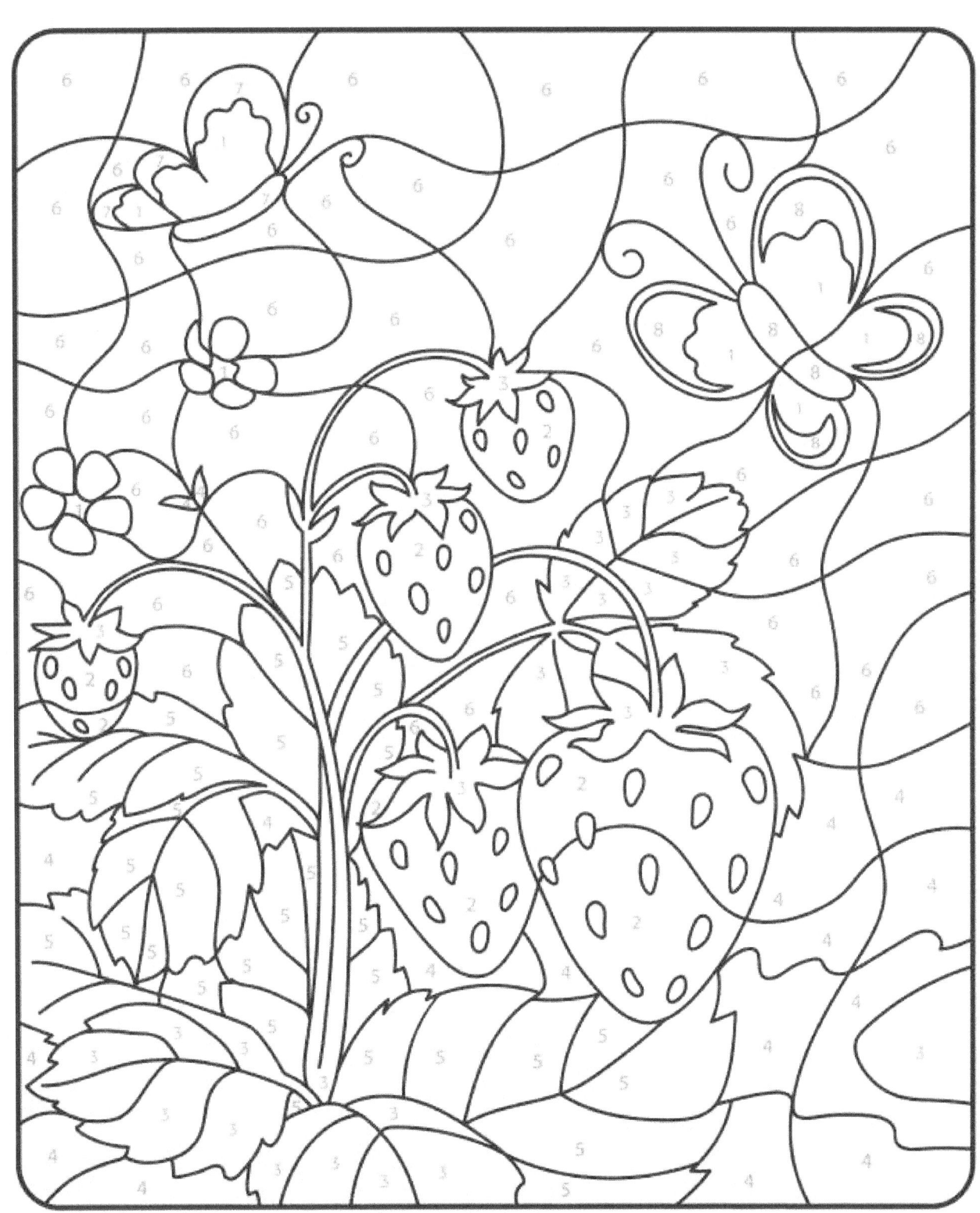

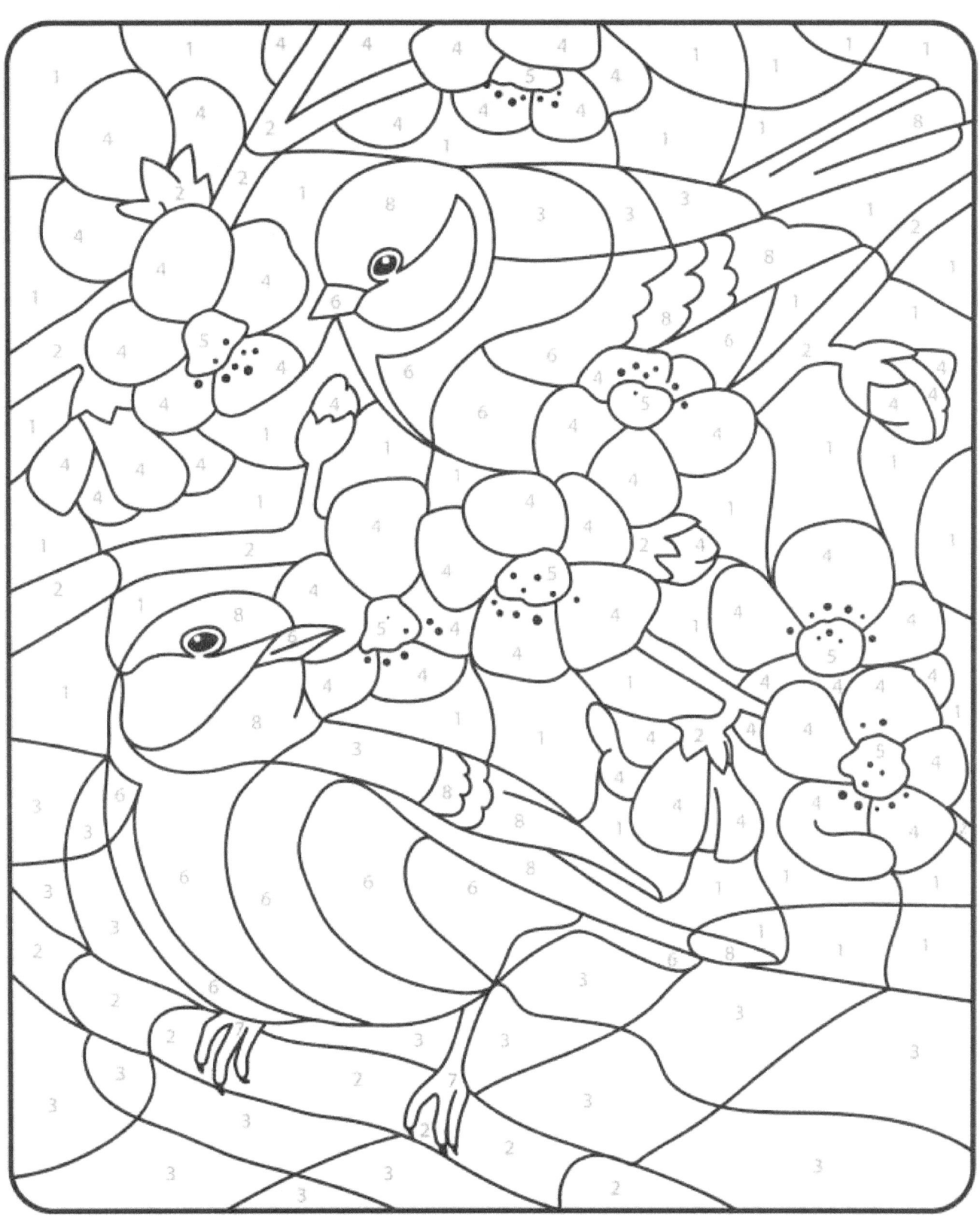

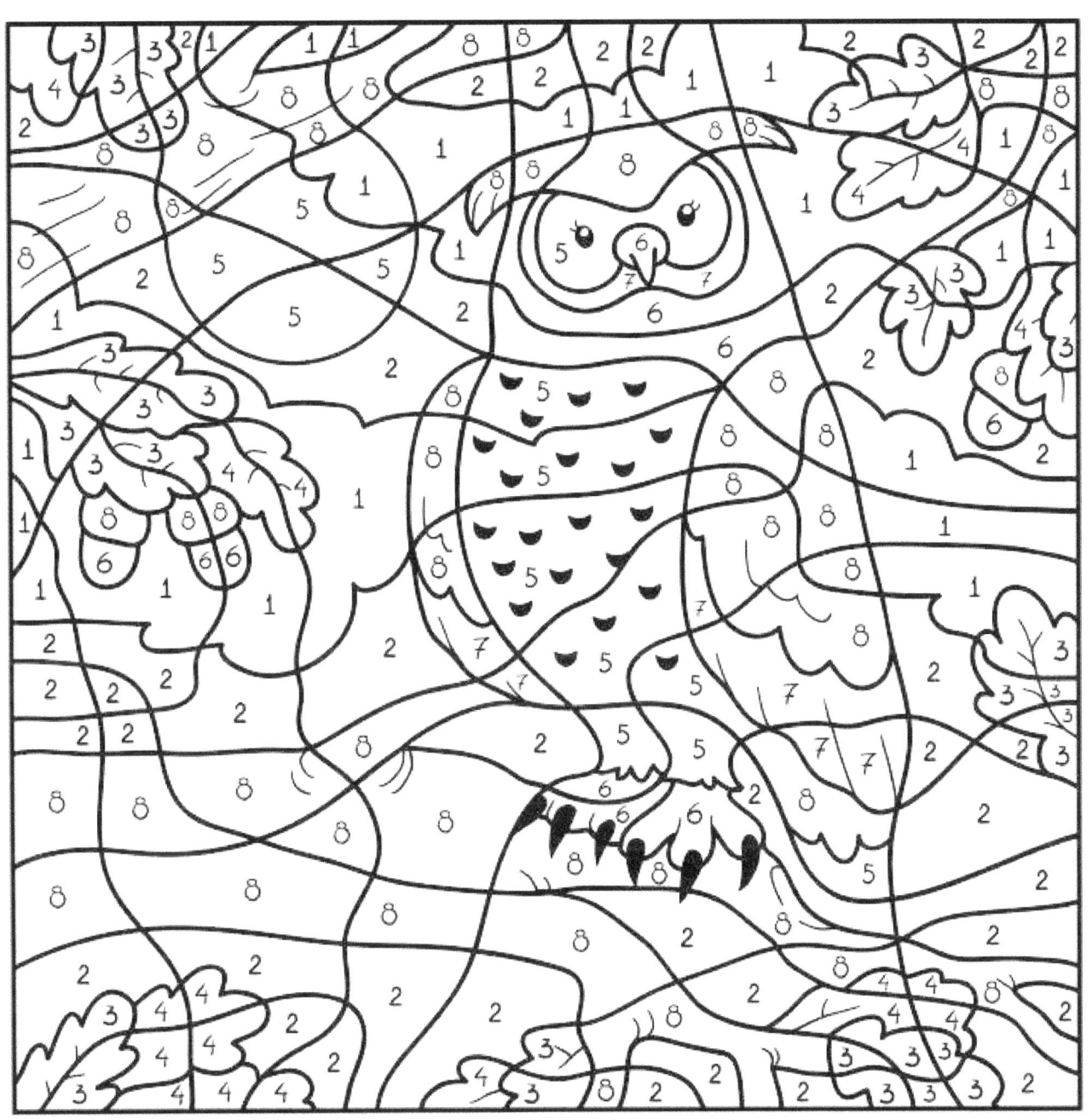

1 - light blue   2 - blue   3 - green   4 - dark green
5 - yellow   6 - orange   7 - gray   8 - brown

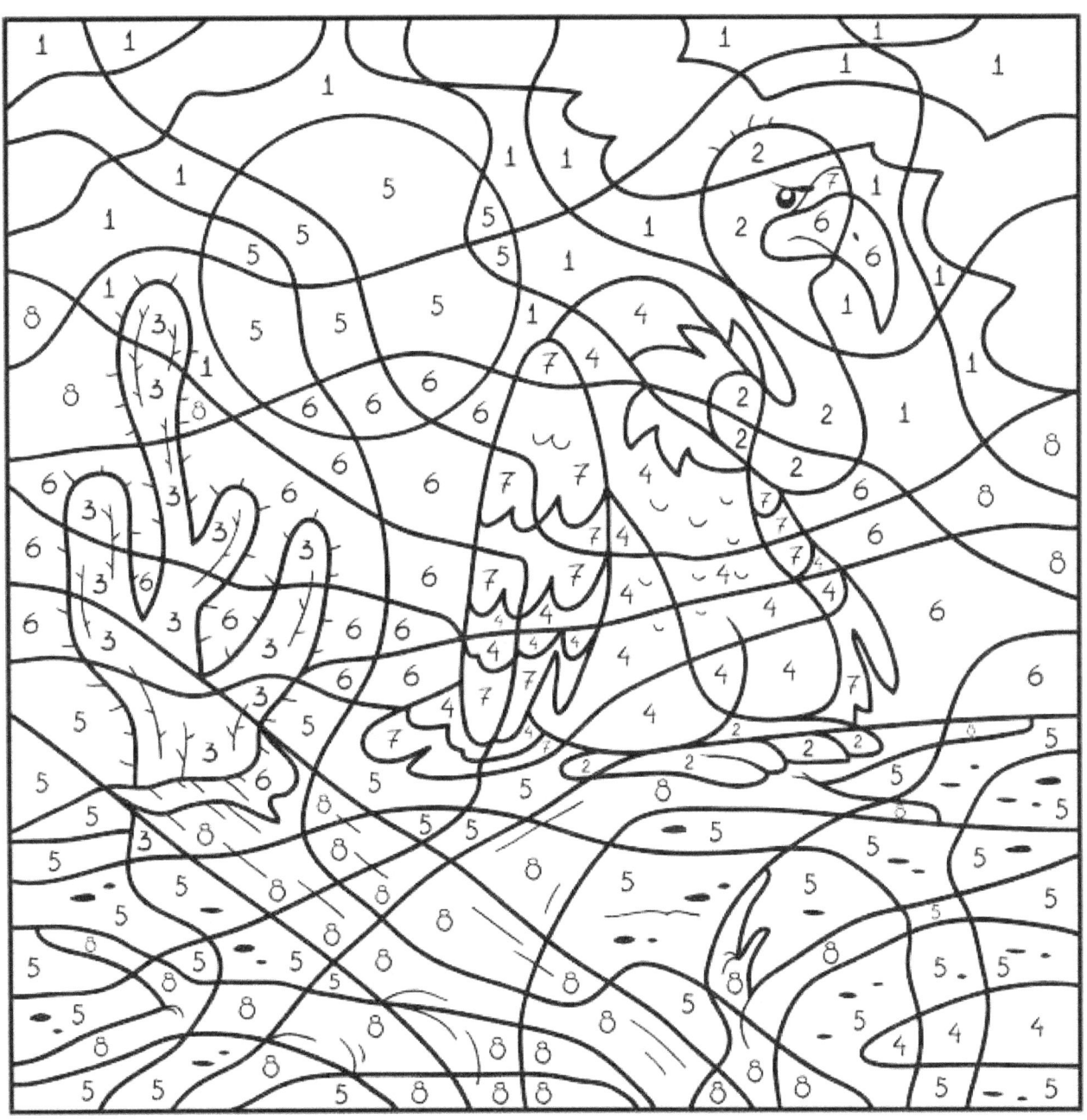

1 - light blue   2 - pink   3 - green   4 - gray
5 - yellow   6 - orange   7 - black   8 - brown

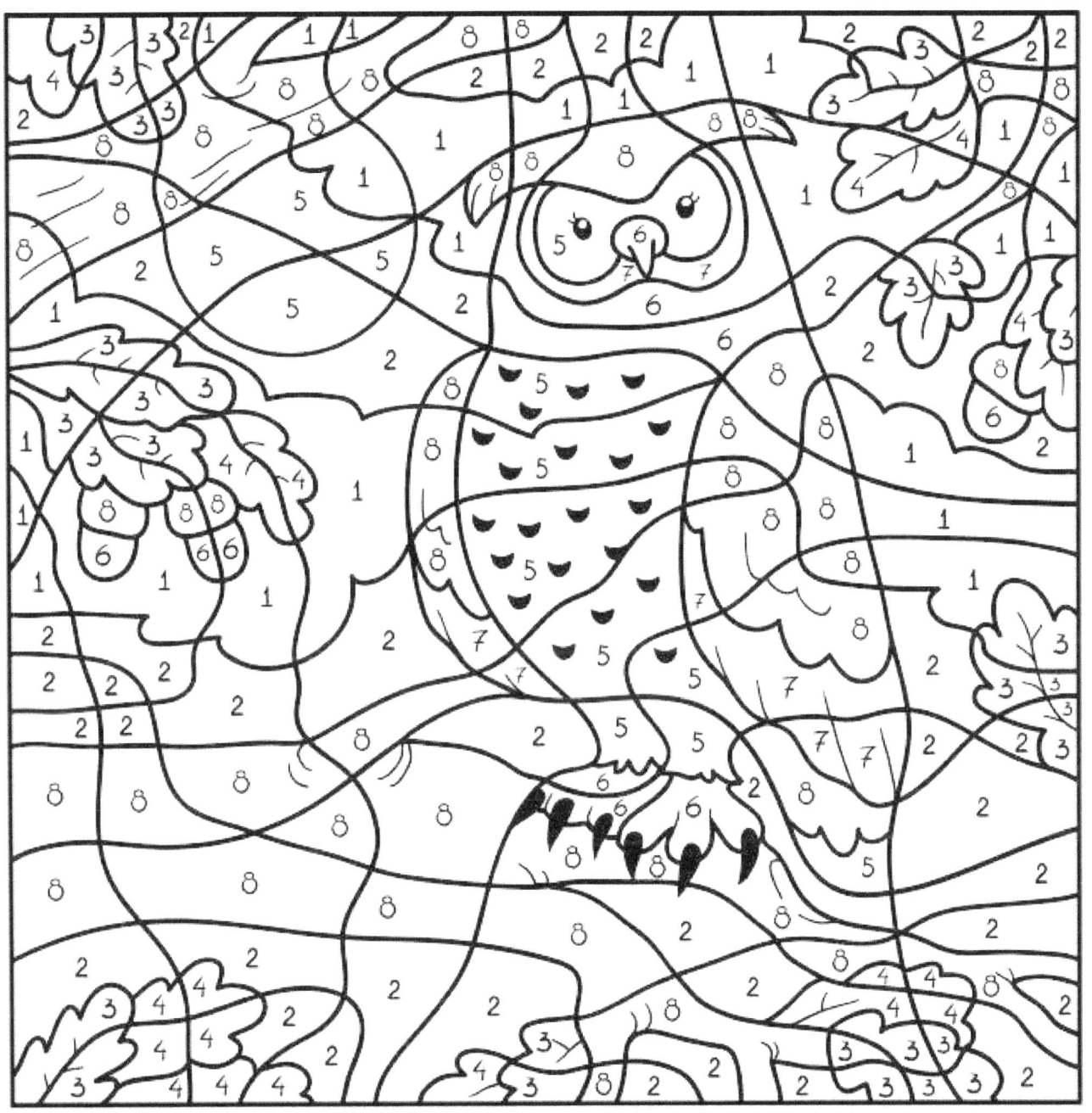

1 - light blue   2 - blue   3 - green   4 - dark green
5 - yellow   6 - orange   7 - gray   8 - brown

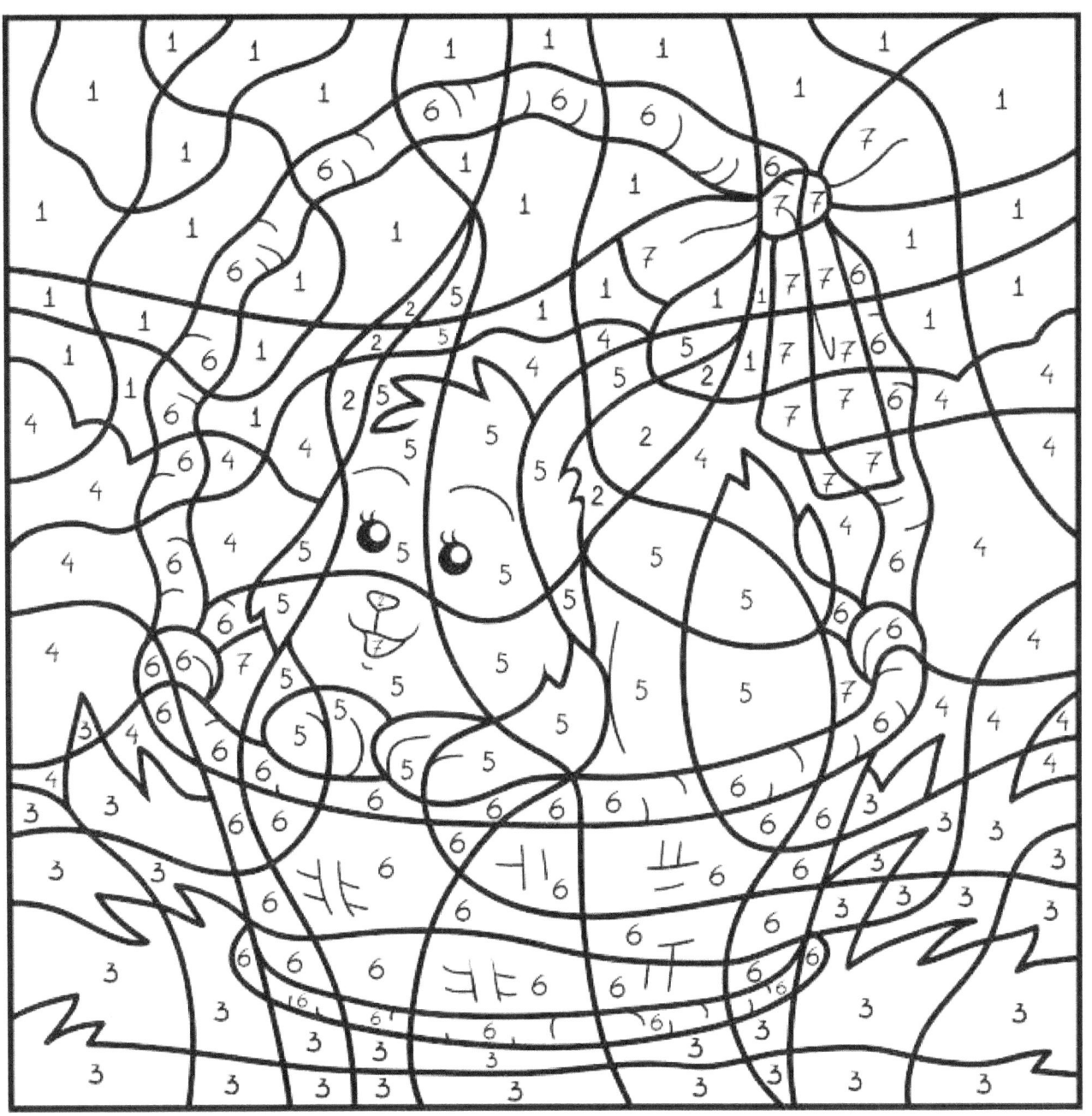

1 - light blue   2 - pink   3 - green   4 - dark green
5 - gray   6 - orange   7 - red

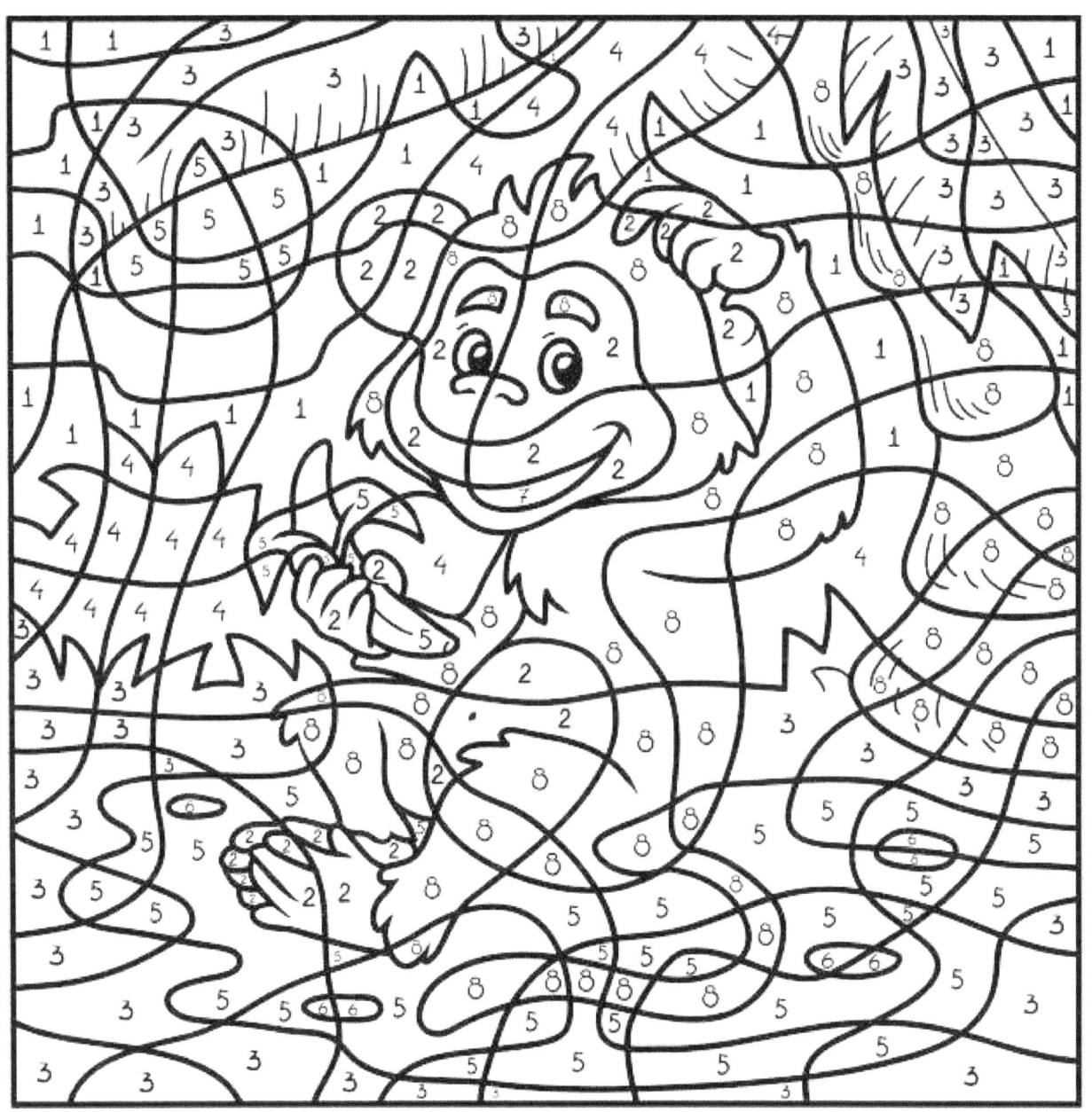

1 - light blue   2 - beige   3 - green   4 - dark green
5 - yellow   6 - gray   7 - red   8 - brown

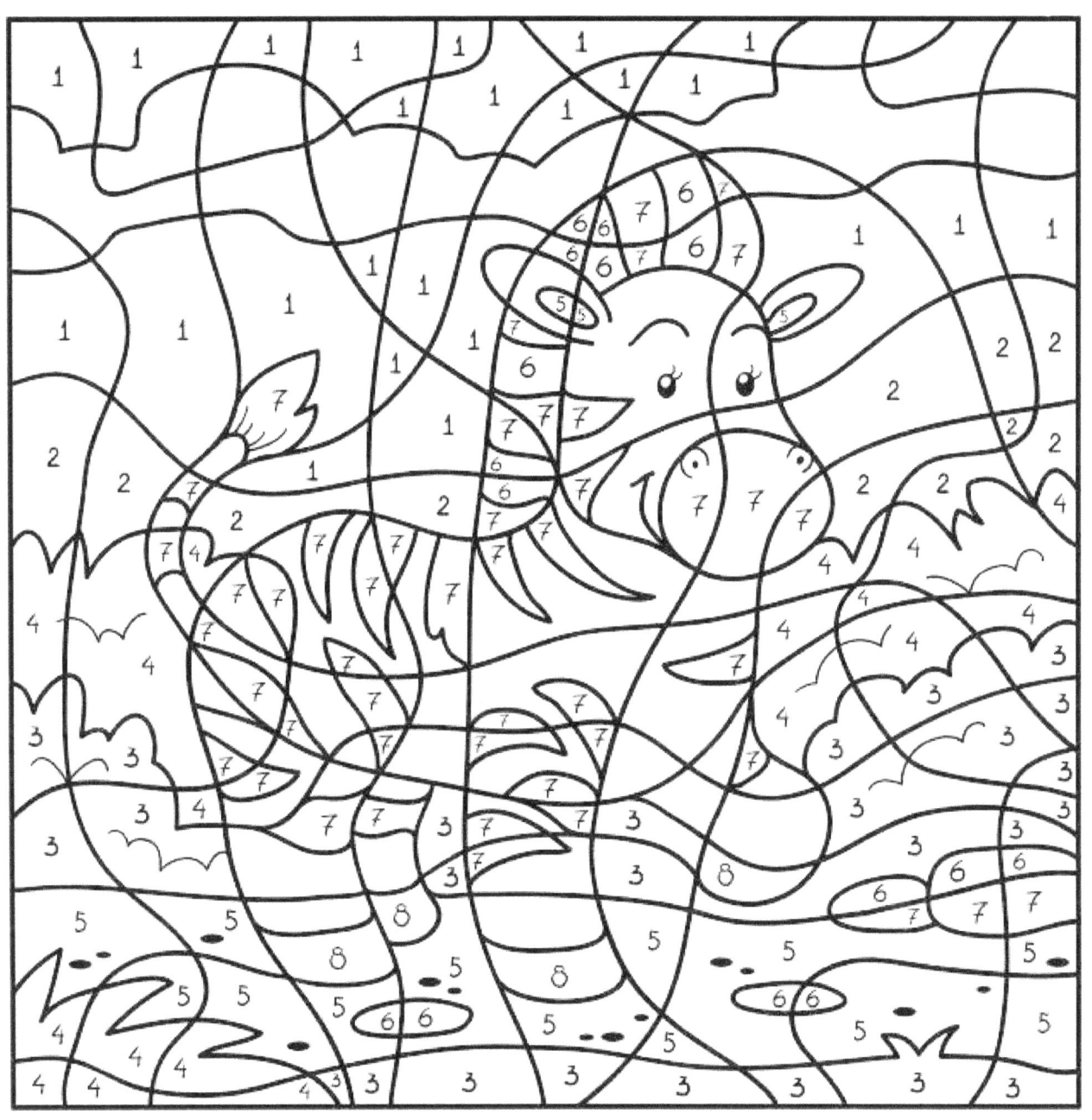

1 - light blue   2 - blue   3 - green   4 - dark green
5 - yellow   6 - gray   7 - black   8 - brown

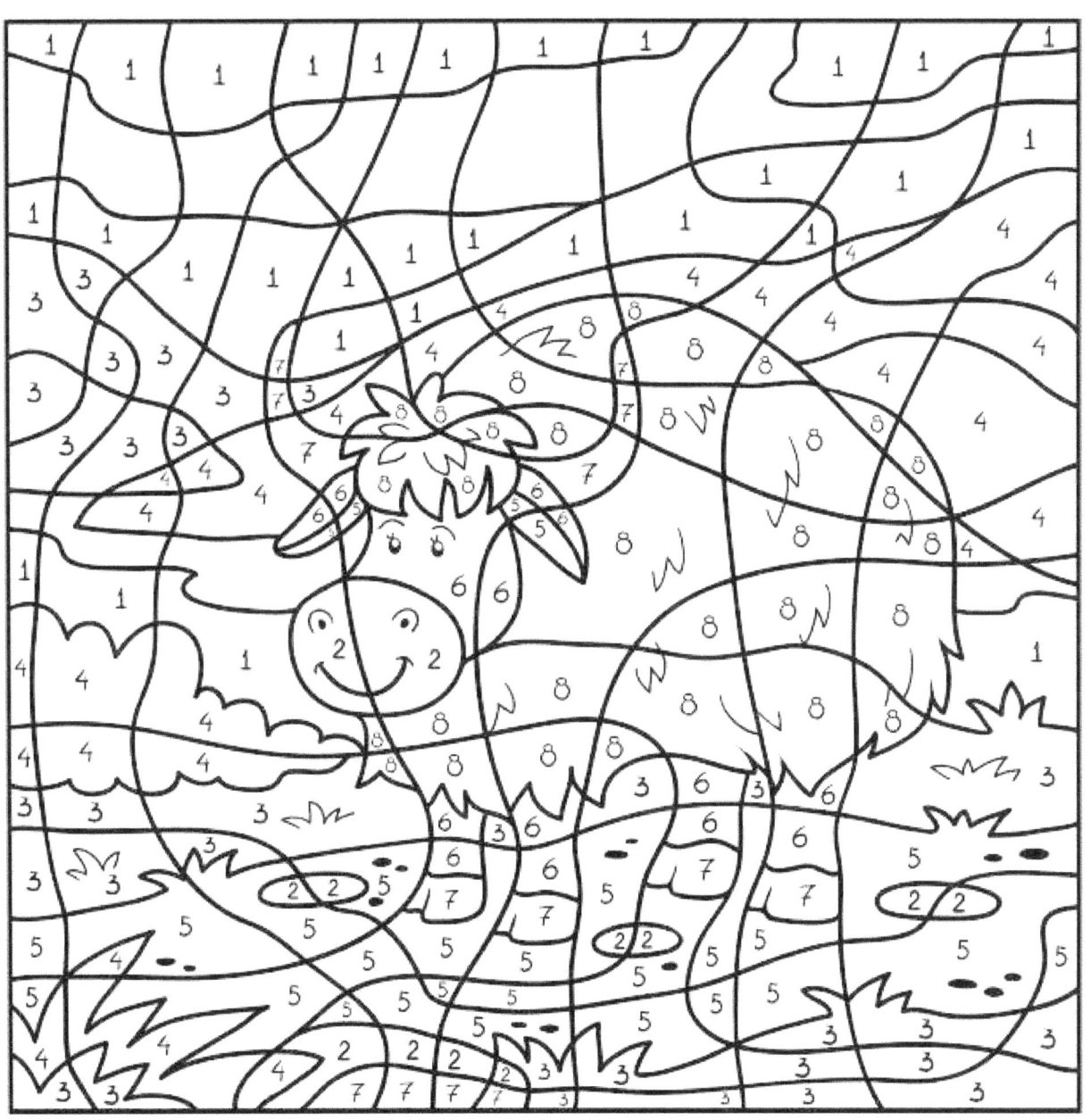

1 - light blue   2 - gray   3 - green   4 - dark green
5 - yellow   6 - orange   7 - black   8 - brown

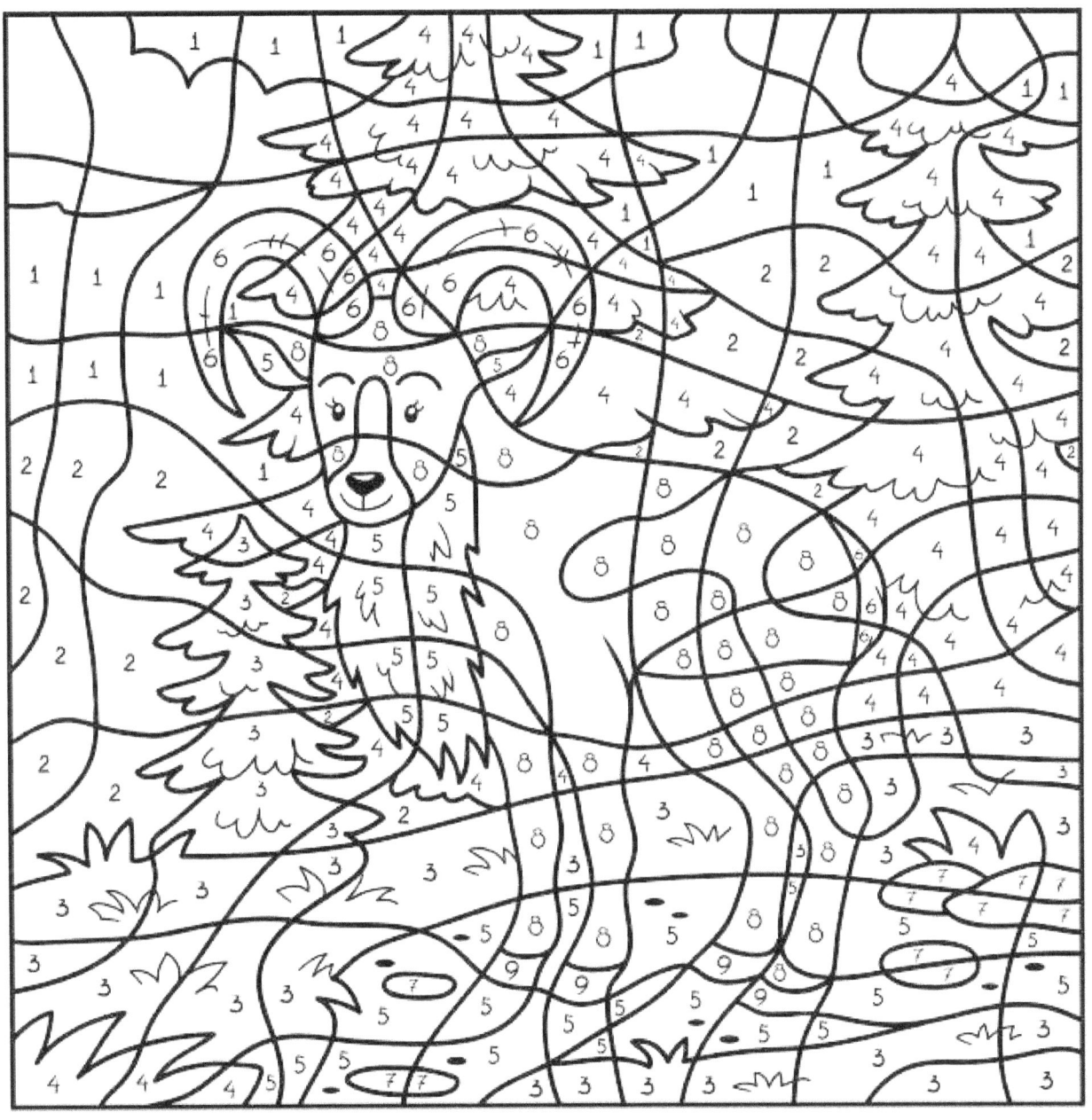

1 - light blue   2 - blue   3 - green   4 - dark green
5 - yellow   6 - orange   7 - gray   8 - brown   9 - black

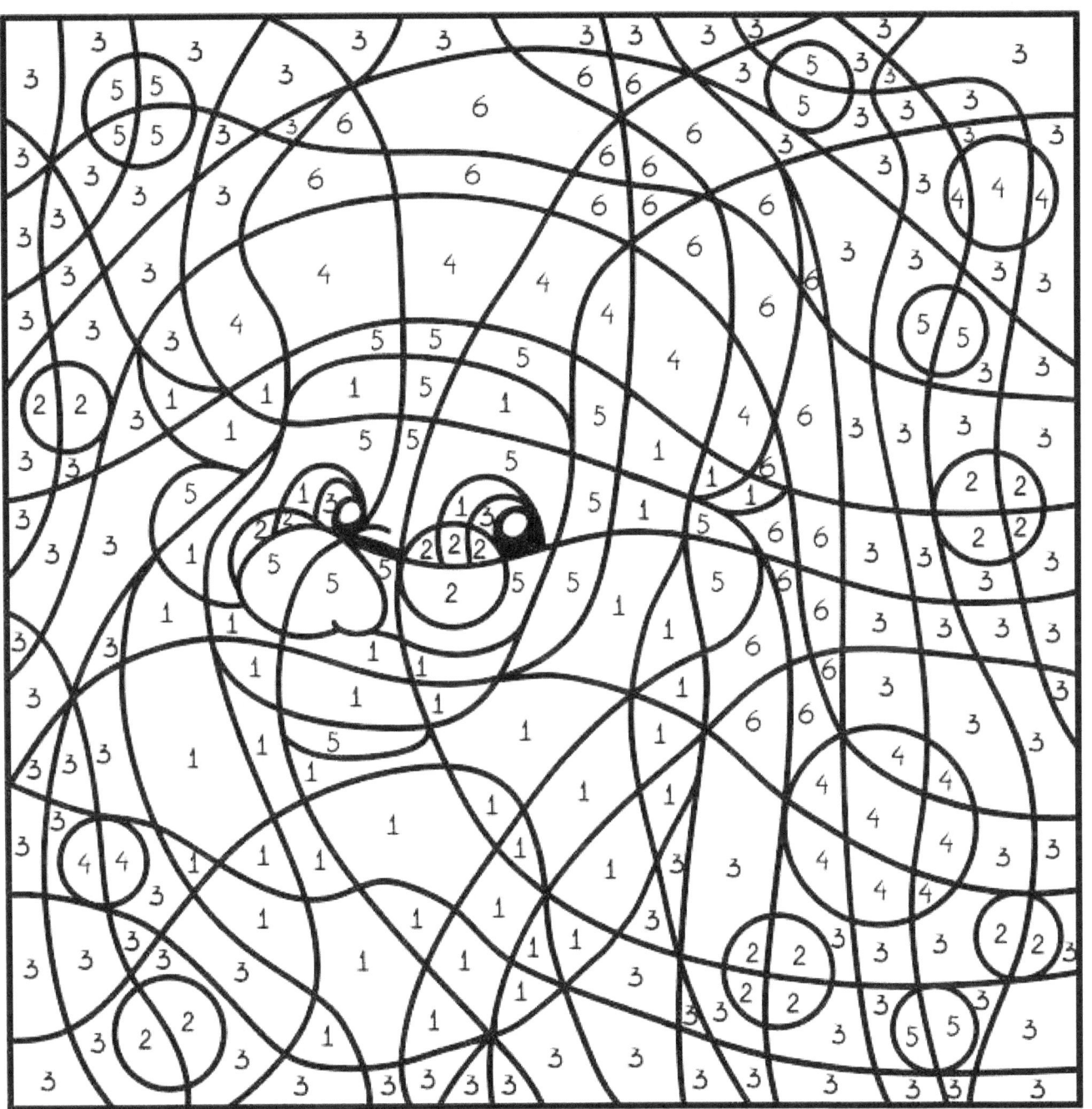

1 - white 2 - light blue 3 - blue 4 - pink 5 - beige 6 - red

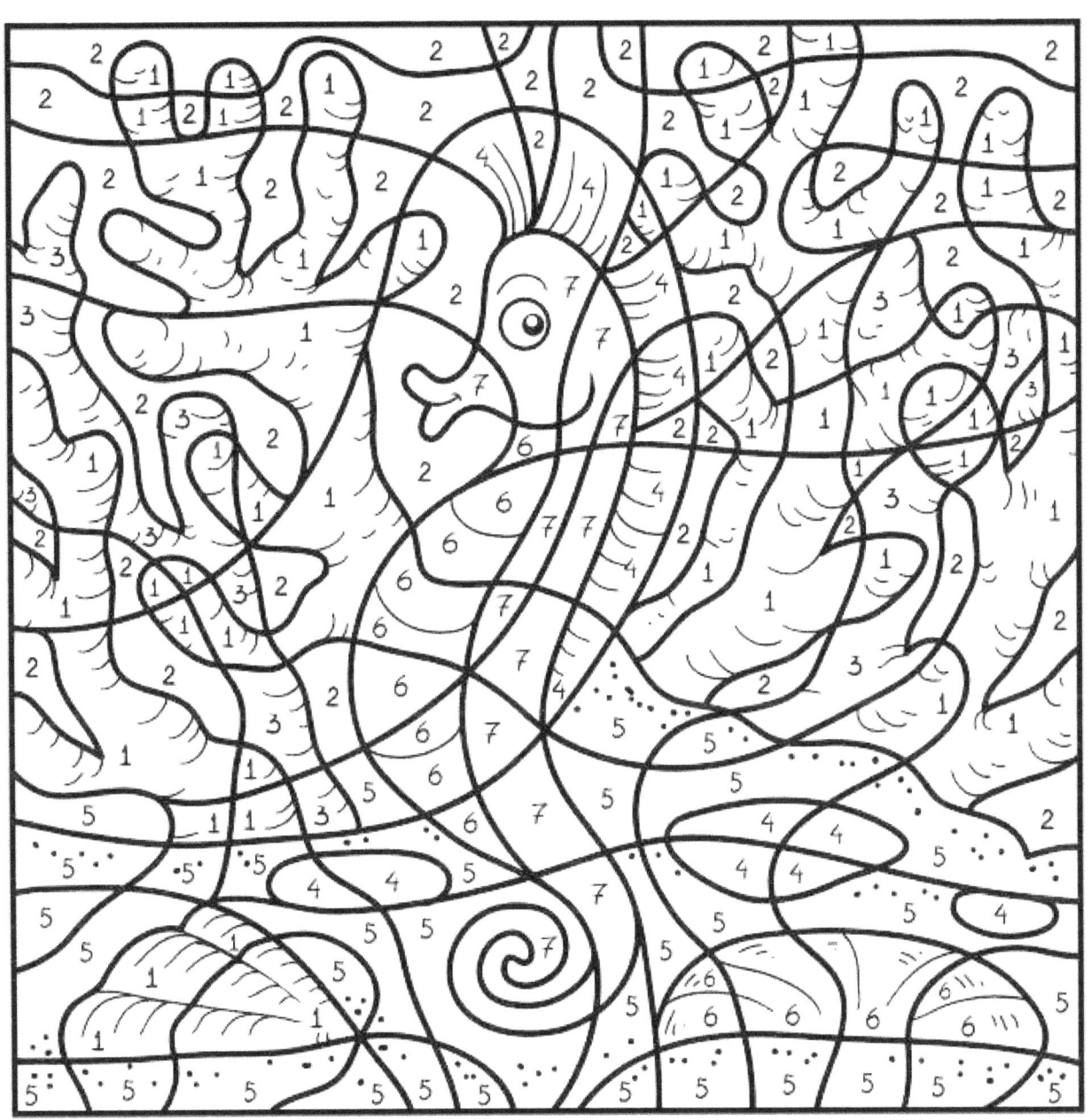

1 - pink   2 - blue   3 - violet   4 - brown
5 - yellow   6 - orange   7 - red

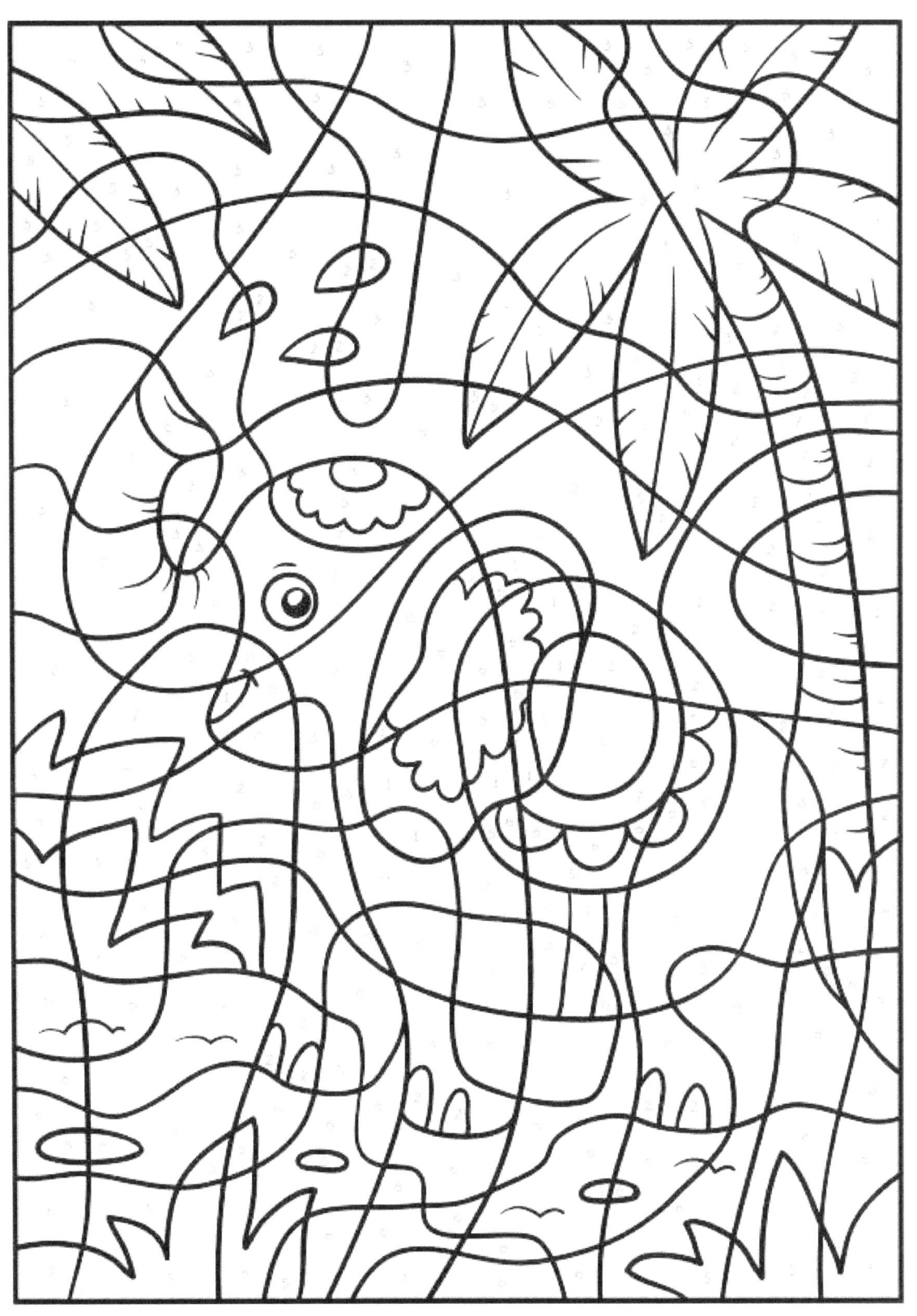

1 - pink   2 - blue   3 - light blue   4 - dark green
5 - green   6 - yellow   7 - orange   8 - gray

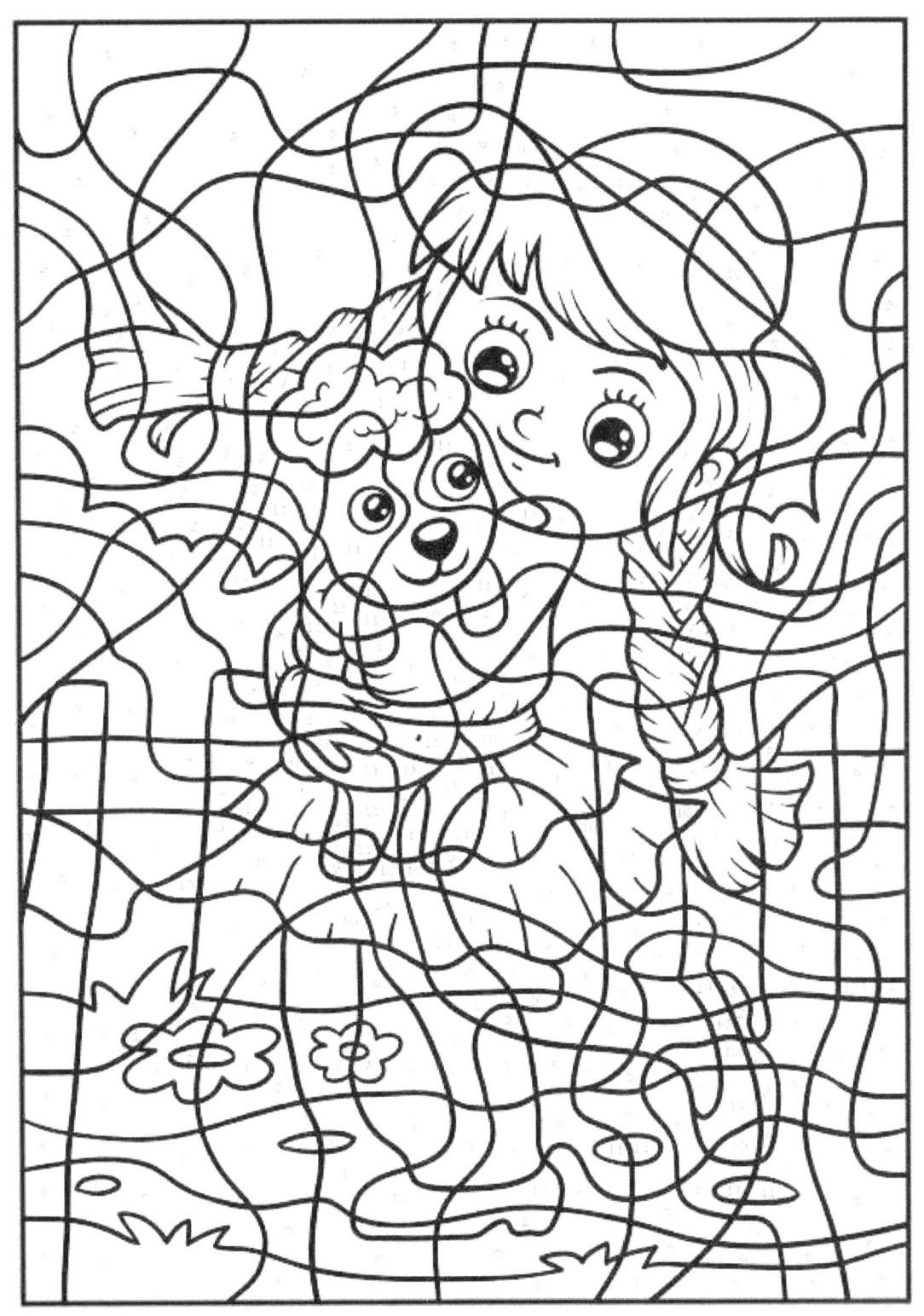

1 - pink   2 - blue   3 - light blue   4 - dark green   5 - green
6 - yellow   7 - orange   8 - beige   9 - brown   10 - red   11 - gray

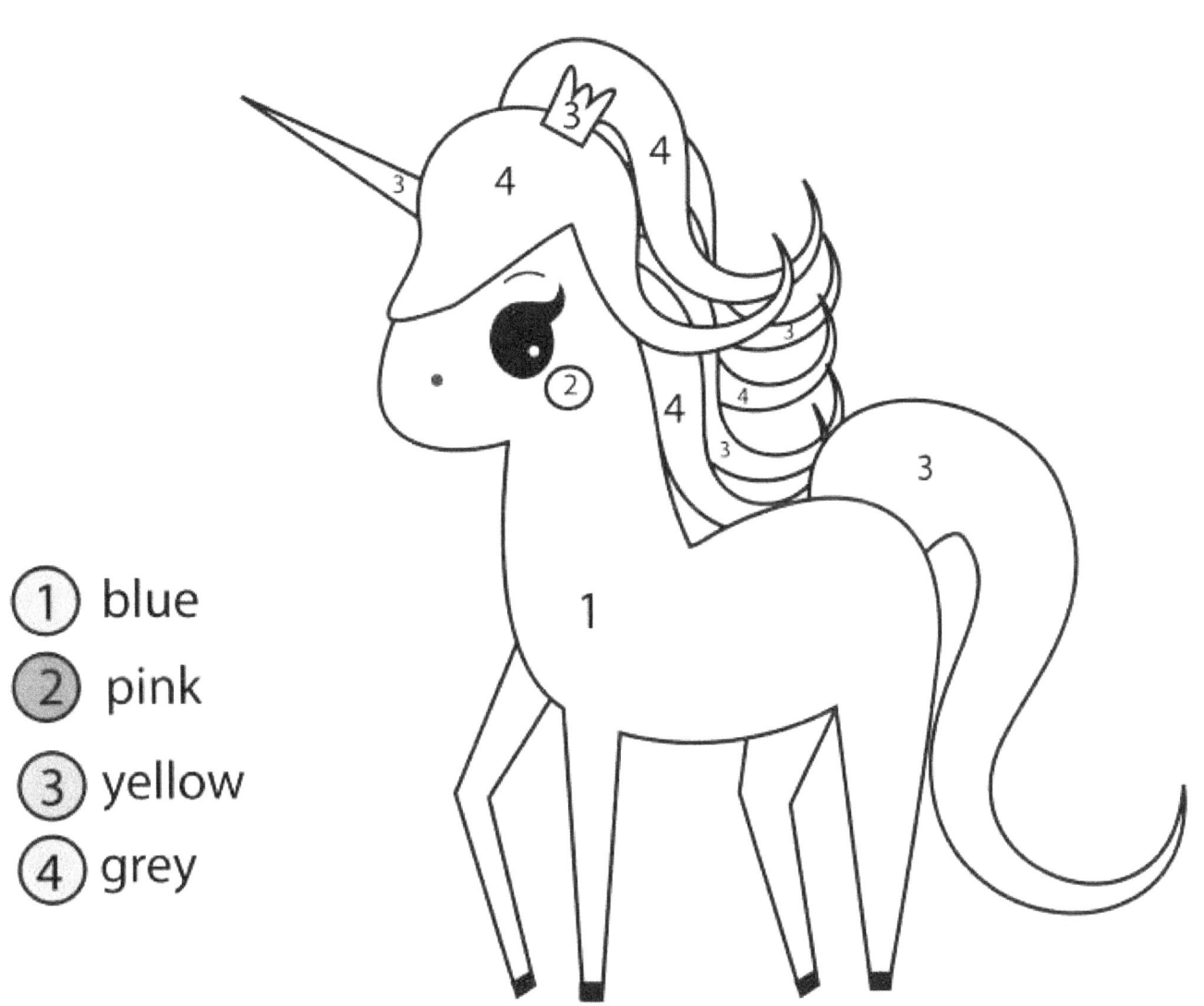

1. blue
2. pink
3. yellow
4. grey

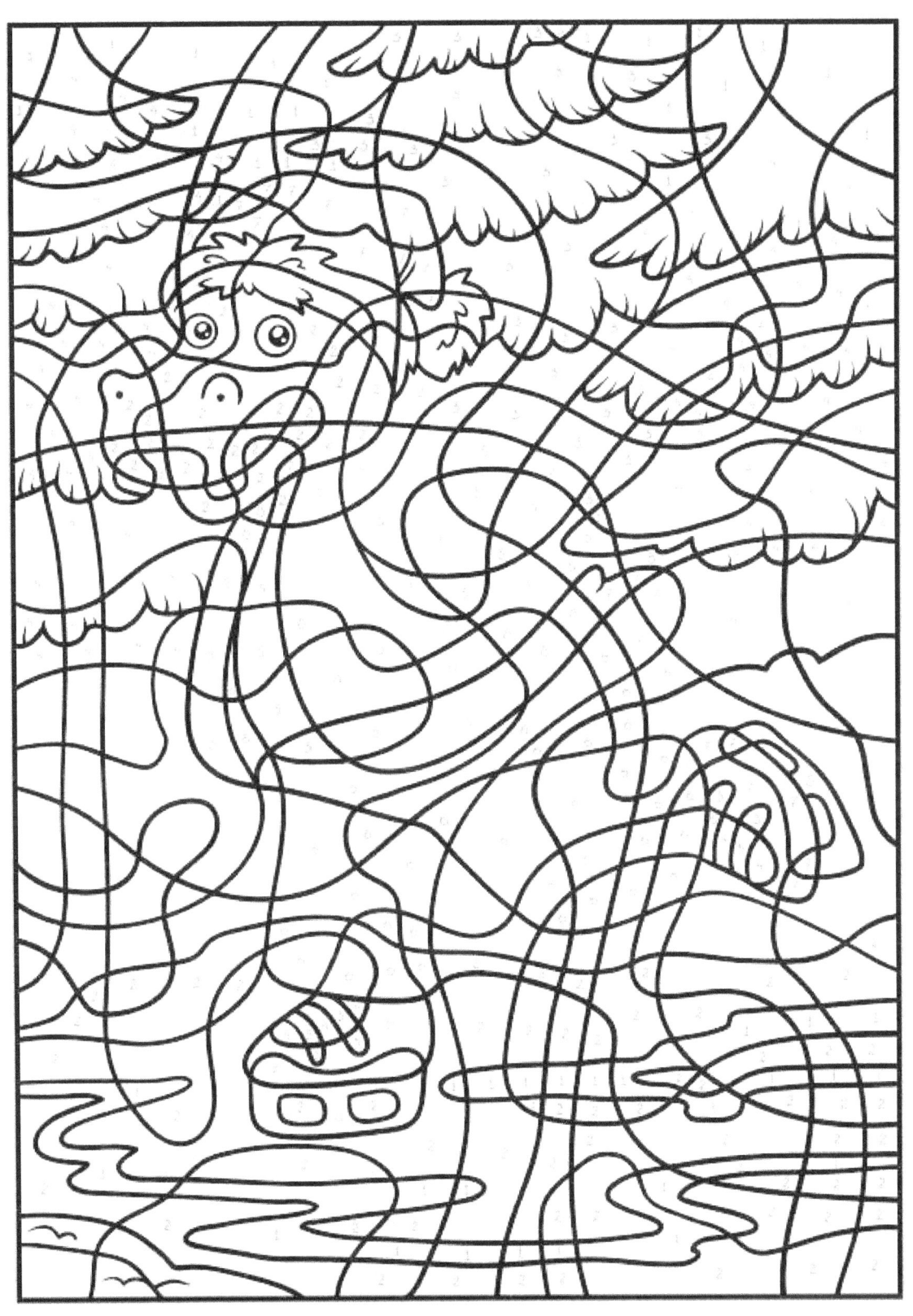

1 - blue 2 - light blue 3 - dark green 4 - green
5 - yellow 6 - brown 7 - red 8 - black